ISBN 0-935493-37-9

Positively Kindergarten:
A Classroom-proven, Theme-based, Developmental Guide for the Kindergarten Teacher

For information, address Modern Learning Press, Rosemont, NJ 08556.

Item # 526.

Positively Kindergarten

A Classroom-proven, Theme-based, Developmental Guide for the Kindergarten Teacher

Beth Lamb, Ph.D. and
Phyllis Logsdon, Ph.D.

Published by Modern Learning Press, Rosemont, NJ 08556

Acknowledgments

To our husbands, W. G. Lamb and Guy W. Logsdon,
who were patient and understanding during this project;

To our mentors,
Dr. Marlow Markert
and
Dr. Martin Burlingame,
who provided a strong foundation for our careers;

To Robert Low and Patricia Coen, our superb editors;

and

MOST OF ALL

To the many five-year-olds who taught us how young children learn.

Contents

A Framework for Teaching 1

★ The Role of a Kindergarten Teacher
Helping to Form the Future
The Teacher Knows. . .
★ The Research Shows. . .
Piaget's Discoveries: The Development of Thought Processes
Gesell's Discoveries: The Developmental Environment
Body Builds
★ Chronological and Behavior Age
The Five-year-old
The Five-and-a-half-year-old
★ Developmental Placement
Do's and Don'ts
Abuses
★ Self-Esteem

The Kindergarten Classroom 14

★ Setting the Stage
The Room
Interest Centers
★ The Visit before the Year Begins
Parent Conferences before School Begins
★ The First Day
The Schedule
The Art of Classroom Management
Quiet Time
Using the Bathroom
Using the Drinking Fountain
Disruptive Behavior
Coping with Tattlers
★ Scheduling
★ The End of the School Year

Planning and Using Unit Themes 29

★ Planning
★ Implementation
★ Suggested Themes

A Day in Kindergarten 33

★ Starting the Day
Saluting the Flag
Taking Attendance
Welcoming Absentees Back
★ Show and Tell
★ The Calendar
Suggested Procedures
★ Discussion
★ Worktime
Introduction of Worktime Activities
★ Outdoor Play
★ Art Activities
Encouraging Young Artists
★ Writing
The Whole Language Approach
★ Reading
The Exposure Method
Field Trips
The Chart Experience
The Daily News
Reading Stories
Listening Centers
★ Mathematics
★ Science
The Science Interest Center
★ Music and Rhythm
Choosing Music
Teaching a Song
Alternatives to the Piano
Listening to Music
Rhythm Time
★ Fingerplays and Activity Poems
★ Snack Time
★ Game Time

Building Partnerships with Other Adults 64

★ Working with Colleagues
★ Working with Administrators
★ Working with Parents
Bulletins
Parents' Meetings
Newsletters
Visiting the Classroom
Occasional Notes
Report Cards
Conferences
★ Working with an Aide

Resources 71

★ Bulletin Boards
★ Unit Themes
★ Fingerplays and Activity Poems
★ Crafts
★ Games

Bibliography 139

Introduction

This book is based on the experiences of many kindergarten teachers, including ourselves. It explains the teaching practices proven to be effective in the classroom as well as the theoretical basis for them. And it offers a wealth of resources—including poems, unit themes, games, and craft projects—you can use in your classroom. We see it as a springboard for your creativity and effectiveness as a kindergarten teacher.

Information from the first sections of this book will help you plan your school year. Then, you'll be able to use information from the resource sections to prepare your weekly lesson plans. You'll probably end up keeping this book open on your desk, where you can refer to it and copy information from it as needed. We hope it will be a valuable aid that will make teaching easier and more rewarding for you.

About Developmental Education

In recent years, there has been renewed support for the teaching methods known as developmental education. This approach to teaching involves matching instructional methods and materials to children's current stage of development, and supporting all four areas of children's development—intellectual, emotional, social, and physical. However, many teachers who recognize the wisdom of this approach have found it difficult to implement, often because of resistance on the part of administrators and, in some cases, parents, who think that "sooner" and "faster" equal "better." In addition, the budget cuts of the 1990s have made it more difficult for many teachers to obtain the appropriate materials and small class sizes that are integral parts of developmental education.

This book provides abundant help for teachers who want to implement a developmental approach. It summarizes the findings of two eminent psychologists, Jean Piaget and Arnold Gesell, whose research confirms the importance of respecting the unique ways in which young children develop and learn. This information can help you convince those who still have doubts about developmental education, and it can help you in your work with students in the classroom.

In addition, this book will help you use specific developmental techniques and materials that have been found to work in kindergarten classrooms year after year. And its extensive collection of ideas and resources—more than can be used in a single year—includes many projects you can create by yourself, without having to purchase expensive, pre-packaged products.

About Kindergarten

Kindergarten students cannot be spectators; they must be involved. The curriculum explained in this book supports learning through the use of interest centers, unit themes, and field trips. Its emphasis is on inquiry, discovery, problem-solving, and decision-making. It is structured yet flexible, and it is based on the characteristics, interests, needs, and accomplishments of the children in the class.

In essence, the kindergarten curriculum is everything that happens to the children from the time they step into the school building until the time they leave. The sum of all their experiences—how they're greeted, how they're instructed, how they work with each other—plays a part in forming their attitudes and motivation long after they've graduated from school.

We therefore believe in creating a positive kindergarten environment—a positive attitude from teachers and positive experiences for the children. Rather than having rigid expectations for achievement, kindergarten teachers need to create a pattern of continuous progress for each child.

This entails paying attention to students' readiness, which we define as the stage at which a child can succeed. Every child is ready to succeed at something; it is the teacher's responsibility to help that happen. A child who is not ready for formal reading instruction, for example, is still ready to be read to, which is a vital step in learning how to read.

About This Book

Chapter One, ***A Framework for Teaching Kindergarten***, explains and supports the developmental approach to education, as well as the developmental characteristics of kindergarten students.

Chapter Two, ***The Kindergarten Classroom***, provides a comprehensive plan for preparing the classroom, planning schedules, and working with children and their parents.

Chapter Three, ***Planning and Using Unit Themes***, presents overviews of numerous themes, along with suggestions for using them to provide positive learning experiences for children.

Chapter Four, ***A Day in Kindergarten***, covers the sequence of experiences that make up a typical school day.

Chapter Five, ***Working with Other Adults***, offers advice on interacting cooperatively and effectively with educators, administrators, and parents.

Resources is a compilation of ideas for bulletin boards, unit themes, fingerplays and activity poems, crafts, and games. These, along with your creativity and enthusiasm, will help you provide consistently fulfilling classroom experiences for your students and yourself.

A Framework for Teaching

Premises

- ★ Early childhood educators teach children, not programs.
- ★ Productive learning is interesting, relevant, satisfying, and fun.
- ★ Reading, writing, and arithmetic are learned; intelligence is developed.
- ★ Children learn most easily from concrete experiences and the use of three-dimensional manipulative materials. (The uninformed call this "play.")
- ★ A rich curriculum is based on the characteristics and traits typical of the age and stage of the children being taught.
- ★ Today is the day that counts. Don't expect to get children "ready" for future experiences. They *are* ready for something, and that's what they should get today. Good todays bring good tomorrows.
- ★ A good kindergarten class has a climate that is relaxed, flexible, and structured for success, without any sense of force or pressure.
- ★ Children's attitudes about life, school, learning, people, and themselves are influenced by the quality of their interaction with others. Educators can have a life-long influence on a child's behavior and values.
- ★ The method of teaching is as important as the subject being taught. Young children should not be humiliated or made to feel apprehensive about learning.
- ★ Educators and parents working together as partners is a formula that results in success for children.

The Role of the Kindergarten Teacher

A child left entirely on his own in a room filled with materials and equipment would find himself in a confusing maze. Kindergarten should be the equivalent of a well-marked road with a clear destination, and it's the teacher who transforms the maze into the road. By subtly structuring the classroom environment with plans and materials, the teacher creates an atmosphere that the child finds positive and motivating.

> *Kindergarten should be the equivalent of a well-marked road with a clear destination, and it's the teacher who transforms the maze into the road.*

Helping to Form the Future

It is during these tender years that children form attitudes about themselves, other people, learning, and the environment. These attitudes will last a lifetime; a teacher's greatest responsibility is to find ways to mold these attitudes in a positive way. If a child is to become a positive adult, the teacher must be a positive person. If the child is to believe there are good and kind people in this world, he or she must view the teacher as a good and kind person. If a child is to be excited about learning, the teacher must dismiss "getting them ready" for some future stage of development and instead create experiences for which they *are* ready, promoting achievement and success without stress. Her ability to do this, and her praise for even the smallest job well done, develops an "I can!" attitude in the child.

The stability and self-confidence of a child who is loved and accepted at home is strengthened when he is accepted and supported in another area—school. The less-fortunate child, one who is less well-loved and accepted at home, has a chance of finding stability and self-confidence through his school experiences. The kindergarten teacher can give this child an essential sense of belonging and the security of knowing what is expected. For this child, school can be a haven, an oasis in a desert of insecurity.

The Teacher Knows . . .

★ Although the teacher seldom sees the adult she helps mold, her long-range concern should be her role in the development of a humane, stable adult, one who can cope with and contribute to a changing culture. She cannot predict what the culture will be in twenty years, so she must concentrate on nurturing problem-solving and decision-making skills.

★ Coping skills need to be developed early, so she makes sure the child's day involves interaction with others, sharing, and taking turns—not very easy for a five-year-old. She knows there must also be contributions to the group—geared to a five-year-old sensibility—so she assigns "helpers" and does nothing she can delegate to the children.

★ She knows the importance of the three R's and will teach them in intellectually honest ways suited to five-year-olds. However, she gives equal importance to fostering self-reliance, self-discipline, self-responsibility, and a sense of right and wrong.

★ She knows children deserve the stability that springs from knowing and understanding what is expected of them, so she plans and adheres to a schedule, makes some rules, and lets the children help decide others. She is consistent with her follow-through.

★ She sees herself as catalyst and guide. Her child-centered classroom is a combination of interest centers, and after the children choose the center that interests them, she goes where she is needed or strolls through the classroom — answering questions, asking questions, promoting problem-solving and giving praise when it has been earned.

★ For the children and for herself, the classroom has a pleasing atmosphere. Displays of the children's work—not just the best—as well as plants and thought-provoking bulletin boards decorate the room.

★ She prepares for each day—in fact, she often overplans. It is a gifted teacher who creates a highly structured environment that is perceived by the children as totally unstructured, as a place where things "just happen." This environment often results in responses of "I just know," when a child is asked, "How do you know that?" The children do not know where or when, in this carefully structured, diverse environment, they absorbed a knowledge or skill for which they were ready.

Displays of the children's work—not just the best—as well as plants and thought-provoking bulletin boards decorate the room.

★ The teacher is professional. Her clothing reinforces the message, "I respect what I am doing."

★ She teaches with an open door, literally and figuratively. The literal open door says, "Come in. Look around. I'm proud of what I'm doing, and I want you to understand it." The figurative open door welcomes visitors, particularly parents, at all times. She knows her program is more qualitative than quantitative, and it must be understood to be appreciated.

★ She is not afraid to answer a question with "I don't know," but she immediately adds, "Let's find out"—a good way to introduce using the library and/or a reference book. Knowing how to find the answers to questions is a hallmark of an educated person.

★ For herself as well as the children, she reads journals, goes to in-service meetings, and attends workshops. Like her charges, she is curious and still learning and growing.

The Research Shows...

There's a variety of authoritative psychological research that offers insights into kindergarten-age children and their typical behavior. Understanding how and why children act the way they do enables you to draw upon their natural patterns and tendencies—to help them learn in ways that are meaningful and appropriate to them.

Piaget's Discoveries: The Development of Thought Processes

In his forty years of research on cognitive development, Jean Piaget revealed concepts that are particularly relevant to kindergarten. They are:

★ A child's intelligence develops as he interacts with the environment and his peers. Children are *active* learners.

★ Children can learn only that for which they are ready. Conversely, they are ready only for that which their past experiences have prepared them.

★ Kindergarten children are not miniature adults; their thinking is unique to their stage of development. It can be characterized as illogical and self-centered and will remain so until an age of approximately seven years.

★ Their natural self-centeredness warps and limits intellectual growth until socialization and confrontation with peers force them to realize that there are others with whom they must learn to cope.

Your role is to guide, question, and provide information.

Making the Most of Piaget's Research

These concepts indicate that the most effective kindergarten curriculum is one which has development of thought process as a major goal. Such a curriculum includes:

★ **Social interaction with peers.** Social interaction and confrontation eventually teach children there are others with needs, wants, and thoughts that can be the same as or different than their own needs, wants and thoughts. This realization helps children understand themselves within a larger framework. Worktime, outdoor play, and any times in the schedule which involve self-selected activities all provide opportunities for this kind of growth.

★ **Learning through concrete experience.** Piaget's research provides ample evidence that young children learn from inquiries, experiments, and discoveries which involve hands-on use of manipulative materials.

★ **A catalytic role for the teacher.** You must structure an environment that enables the children to discover reality through their endeavors. Your role is to guide, question, and provide information.

A developmental curriculum *does not* include:

★ **Using workbooks to teach.** Workbooks present a two-dimensional representation of what children need to experience in three dimensions. They allow for neither trial-and-error nor discovery, both of which are essential for learning.

★ **Rigid standards for content.** By rigid standards, we mean those criteria which require children to master particular goals at a specific age. The program must be structured to fit the needs of each individual—a task easily accomplished with the use of interest centers.

★ **Labeling children as academically behind, on target, or ahead.** Each child is ready for something. Our job is to fulfill that need.

★ **Grouping by scholastic aptitude.** Piaget's research found that, like water finding its level, children seek their levels by selecting appropriate materials and companions—grouping themselves in a natural manner. In addition to giving the teacher valuable clues, such natural grouping can be expected to breed positive experiences, positive development, and ultimately a positive self-image.

Gesell's Discoveries: The Developmental Environment

At about the same time that Piaget was studying cognitive development, Arnold Gesell was researching the neuro-motor development of children. He was curious about how children behave and how they perceive the world around them. The basic concepts derived from Gesell that are relevant for kindergarten education are:

Each child is ready for something. Our job is to fulfill that need.

★ **Behavior is a function of structure.** The human organism develops in a predictable pattern with an unchanging sequence, but with individually unique timing. Observable behavior results from a combination of the stage of development, physical build, and interaction with the environment.

★ **Each child has a time-clock—a rate of growth—that is right for him.** It is nature-ordained and develops in its own time. It can't be changed or rushed and should not be ignored.

★ **Neuro-motor growth is not a straight line, "better and better" proposition.** Growth is a rising spiral of swings from stages of equilibrium to stages of disequilibrium.

★ **There are six developmental stages experienced by growing children.** In infants these stages last but a few weeks; they gradually lengthen until age seven, at which point the stages last a year. Each stage has characteristic social, emotional, physical, and mental behavior.

More information about ages and stages of development can be found in the book *School Readiness* by Frances L. Ilg, Louise Bates Ames, and Jacqueline Haines.

★ **Chronological age does not guarantee a level of development consonant with that age.** Children are like fingerprints. A lot about them may seem alike and we can make valid generalizations, but each child's

> *What relief it is to know the changes from five to five and one-half are to be expected, not condemned!*

personal time-clock is unique.

Making the Most of Gesell's Discoveries

These concepts indicate that the most effective kindergarten curriculum is one that is attuned to children's stages of development. A developmental environment for kindergarten includes:

★ **Work with materials that enable the expansion of large and small muscle development.** With few exceptions, children do not read until they have well-coordinated bodies. Time on a well-equipped playground is desirable.

★ **Use of resource books.** You will enhance your effectiveness by studying Gesell's literature that discusses the characteristics of the ages you are teaching. What relief it is to know the changes from five to five-and-one-half are to be expected, not condemned!

★ **Teacher empowerment.** After studying characteristics of the age you are teaching and getting to know the children in your care, *only you* can plan a program which is appropriate. Resource books, in-service meetings, and current literature will be all the help your creativity needs.

★ **Realistic expectations.** Because children alternate between stages of equilibrium and disequilibrium, you can't expect consistent progress at a steady rate.

★ **Alternate activities.** Since kindergarten children tire easily, they need a schedule which alternates between busy and calm activities.

★ **Behavior age as the gauge.** If a child's behavior is appropriate for an age younger than his chronological age, he may be overplaced in school. Research from the Gesell Institute indicates " . . . children should start school and be subsequently promoted on the basis of their developmental age rather than their age in years." Depending on administrative policy and parental agreement, you might want to recommend what the Gesell Institute calls the "gift of time"—placing the child with peers who have reached a similar developmental age.

A developmental environment for kindergarten does *not* include:

★ **Mandatory pencil and paper work.** Such activities can be frustrating to children with the typical small-muscle development of a five, and excruciating to a five-and-one-half at the reversal stage. If included at all, the experience should be optional.

★ **Large crayons.** These are usually used because they're hard to break, but small crayons are more suited to small hands. If both kinds of crayons are on the shelf, children will choose the small ones.

★ **Teacher's manuals that call all the shots.** These materials are hardly child-centered. A step-by-step procedure that dictates everything you say and do makes for a pretty dull day. It accomplishes little more than atrophying your originality, creativity, and responsiveness.

★ **Rigid expectations.** A program dictated by scope and sequence cannot be individualized—it ignores the child's nature-ordained time-clock.

★ **An all-busy or all-quiet program.** Too much activity or quiet will be tiring and eventually repress motivation.

★ **Overplacement.** It is unrealistic to expect a behavioral four-year-old to live up to the same adjustment as a five-year-old. If you must teach a behavioral four, alter your expectations.

Body Builds

The more a teacher knows about children, the easier it is to help them. Many times a child's body type furnishes some clues.

The study of body types—or constitutional psychology—first appeared in William Sheldon's *Varieties of Temperament.* Early in their research, the Gesell Institute found they were replicating Sheldon's findings; they dropped their research and accepted his.

At first we found this concept hard to accept, but as we observed children, we saw its validity. We suggest that you review the following information, which is based on *Is Your Child in the Wrong Grade?* and *Why Am I So Noisy? Why Is She So Shy?* by Louise Bates Ames, and observe your students. Then reach your own conclusions.

The more a teacher knows about children, the easier it is to help them.

Three "types" of body builds and related characteristics have been identified. Each person actually represents a unique combination of these three different components, but in most people one component seems to predominate.

Mesomorphs tend to be squarely built, with broad shoulders and thick arms and legs. They have strong muscles and are active, vigorous children who love exercise and sports. They often emerge as the leaders in a group of children and are highly competitive. Such children may find it difficult to sit still and do fine-motor tasks for long periods of time. Frequent opportunities for exercise, rest, and recreation help.

Ectomorphs are more likely to be tall and skinny, with flat chests and poorly muscled arms and legs. Their behavior shows restraint, inhibition, over-sensitivity, shyness, and sometimes even a desire for concealment. They often are interested in and good at academic activities. Some extra encouragement and support may be needed to help them feel comfortable in school, while reprimands or criticism may be more upsetting to them than to other children.

Endomorphs have round, soft bodies with short arms and legs and plump hands and feet. They love food and people, and in school are usually good-natured and sociable. However, they may not try as hard nor do as well as parents and teachers think they should. Adult efforts to stimulate more competitiveness or outstanding performance in kindergarten are likely to do little good and are not advised.

Chronological and Behavior Ages

Behavior ages and chronological ages don't always jibe.

The Five-year-old

Fives tire easily and will cry when they're angry, tired, or can't have their way. They may slam the door, or stamp a foot, but they are usually delightful, loving children.

Five is a smooth, wonderfully pleasant stage of development. Fives are anxious to please; they want to conform. They are sociable and ready for short periods of group activity. They need and profit from the security of knowing what to expect. Fives like to hold an adult's hand when they're feeling insecure. Although they have good body control, their large muscle development is coming along better than that of their small muscles. They like to climb and some can skip. Their large muscles still need a lot of outdoor play, preferably in a well-equipped playground. They have good eye-hand coordination. They like block building, sand, clay work, painting, cutting and pasting—all activities which will contribute to small muscle development.

Some can be expected to lace their shoes but tying may still be a way off. Fives are careless about their clothes.

At the table, Fives dawdle but usually enjoy their food. Breakfast is the poorest meal. Most like meat, potatoes, and fruit. Many will balk at casserole dishes; they do not like mixtures.

Fives will nap maybe two times a week and need a seven or eight o'clock bedtime. They like a pre-sleep activity such as hearing a story and they like to take a toy to bed. If they wake at night to toilet, they may have a hard time going back to sleep. Dreams are mostly about bears or wolves.

Fives usually have one elimination a day, after a meal, and may need help wiping. Bladder control has developed but some children need an occasional reminder, especially when involved in an activity.

Their health is good—maybe one or two colds a year. Stomach aches are real but usually connected with food the child dislikes. It is not unusual to have a "bellyache" before a bowel movement.

Fives will reveal tension by nail-biting, thumb-sucking, and eye-blinking.

Emotionally they can be serene, serious, and realistic. They are dependent on adults, will cooperate with them, and *love* their families.

Fives tire easily and will cry when they're angry, tired, or can't have their way. They may slam the door, or stamp a foot, but they are usually delightful, loving children.

Fives love to be read to and will hear a favorite story over and over.

This is not a fearful age but there are concrete fears—being hurt, the dark, thunder, sirens, and mom not being home.

Fives are very self-centered. They think the world revolves around them. As intelligence develops, children will realize they are a spoke of the wheel, not the hub, and that the other children are here to stay, so they might as well get along with them. This cycle of intelligent growth is not completed until approximately age seven, but the kindergarten experiences of active learning, sharing, and taking turns help them accept this somewhat unwelcome reality.

All in all, you are dealing with a happy child who is in an enjoyable stage. Enjoy! It's the calm before the storm.

The Five-and-a-half-year-old

Teachers and parents may be asking, "What happened to this wonderful child?!" Another stage of development happened. The fives' nervous system has undergone a tremendous spurt of growth and the smoothness has temporarily left their bodies. They are not the angels we enjoyed. They are inconsistent, sassy, and brash, and have a very hard time making any kind of decision. "Yes, let's go see granny," they say, and by the time you get to the car, they've decided "I don't want to go." At five, they might have known right and left. Now they probably don't. They love you or hate you. They had been pretty well coordinated, but now they can't trust their own bodies. When writing names or numbers, Five-and-one-halfs will very likely reverse, writing the name so that it can be read in a mirror. They want to ride a bike but are very clumsy. Eye-hand coordination is awkward.

They still need a bedtime of seven or eight, still like to be read to before sleep, and still take a toy to bed. When undressing, they're likely to throw clothes all over the room.

Five-and-one-halfs have more colds than Fives and will complain of foot, head, and stomach pain. This is the typical age for whooping cough and chicken pox. They reveal tension by putting hand to mouth, throat-clearing, nail-biting, thumb-sucking, hair-chewing, and pencil-biting.

> *Five-and-a-half-year-olds can be very moody.*

Crying is loud and angry, and temper tantrums can accompany this age. They can be very moody. They call people names, threaten, hit, and can be destructive. If sent to their room for punishment, they may break things.

They are very fearful of sounds, being lost, and sleeping alone, especially if the bedroom is upstairs. They worry about losing mother. They dream that things are in the bed, things like wild animals. When waking from this sort of dream, they'll run to the parents' room.

A child's placement in school—not his admittance—should be gauged by behavior age instead of chronological age.

All in all this can be a difficult stage for the children and those around them. Their lives are made simpler with a routine they can expect. They manage better when given advance warning about changes in schedules or events.

For some reason, they listen better if instructions and requests are sung to them. At this stage, almost anything is good if it works.

This too will pass.

Developmental Placement

A chronological five may be out of bounds, always on the go, not anxious to please, and consistently wild. That behavior is typical of a four-year-old; we've found that fives with the behavior of fours do not profit from being placed with truly behavioral fives.

If a five is ambivalent, sometimes like a five, scaring easily and full of fears, he is behaving like, and will be more comfortable with, four-and one-half year old children. A child's placement in school—not his admittance—should be gauged by behavior age instead of chronological age. It takes some doing, but the practice has become widespread.

Many schools practice developmental placement, usually based on the Developmental Observation Assessment that grew from the research of Arnold Gesell and his colleagues, Frances Ilg and Louise Bates Ames, during their years at the Yale Clinic of Child Development. This approach to education requires an administrative decision, and parents must often be properly informed and make a change in their thinking in order to see its value.

We worked in one of the first schools in the country to use developmental placement, where developmental placement was *used, not abused.* We will discuss abuses later.

We learned that when properly implemented, developmental placement:

★ Practically eliminated discipline problems;

★ Forced us into individualized instruction because of a wider range of achievement;

★ Resulted in children who loved school and professionals who enjoyed their work.

Do's and Don'ts

Some general "do's"...

★ If you want to use the Gesell Developmental Assessment, you or someone in your school system must take an intensive three-day workshop to learn how to administer and evaluate the assessment.

★ Count your first twenty-five tests as practice.

★ If possible, work with another examiner. Your self-confidence will build a little faster.

★ Every year, a month or two before the assessment, educate your parents at a meeting to explain developmental concepts.

★ Make placement recommendations with a committee that includes your administrator.

And some guidelines to follow. . .

★ **Developmental placement should involve nothing other than placing a child with other children of the same behavior age.** If a five is behaving like a four, he is going to be more comfortable and consequently more productive if placed with fours. If placed with fives, he may be overwhelmed and appear to be a misfit or at best make the grade at the price of a skewed development.

★ **Developmental placement practically mandates individualized instruction that is non-pressured and open-ended.** A six-year-old may be developmentally five and if that's the case, he belongs with fives in kindergarten. There should be no reason why he cannot accomplish as much academically in kindergarten as he would in first grade. In other words, depending on basic abilities and readiness, it is possible for a six-year-old who is developmentally five to accomplish more in kindergarten than a six-year-old who is developmentally six and properly placed in first grade.

★ **Although a developmental assessment provides valuable information about a child's behavior age, weight should be given to the information provided by a previous teacher and the parent.** Flexibility should accompany the decision. If, during the year, the teacher thinks a child might function better elsewhere, that child should be re-evaluated and placed at the level that best suits him.

> *If, during the year, the teacher thinks a child might function better elsewhere, that child should be re-evaluated and placed at the level that best suits him.*

Abuses

One abuse of developmental placement has been its use as an admission tool. No child should ever be denied admittance to a school. It is the responsibility of educators to provide the proper atmosphere and programs for children. A child's intelligence develops as he interacts with his peers so *he must be with other children.* If a school does not have a pre-K or a developmental first grade, two years in a kindergarten with a wide range of activities is a satisfactory alternative.

Forcing the issue is also an abuse of the concept. You might win the battle but lose the war! In public schools, where parents have no choice as to where their children attend school, parents should have the final say about placement. If parents are coerced into a decision, their unhappiness will be apparent to the child, which defeats the purpose of helping a child be happy with his school situation. In private schools that parents choose for their children, the school's policy can be known and then accepted or rejected.

Developmental placement should not be used as an excuse to protect a child from an improper curriculum. One of the abuses perpetrated under the name "developmental placement" has been to keep a child in kindergarten or to place him in developmental first because the kindergarten teacher knew the curriculum was something he would not be able to handle. Wrong! That involves an entirely different issue. In such cases, the curriculum (probably program-centered) should be changed to a child-centered curriculum which allows self-pacing and continuous progress.

Five-year-olds can't risk failure and should not be compared to one another. It's a good idea to stay away from games, races, and contests with winners and losers.

Self-esteem

The interaction between children and their environment has a profound effect on the rest of their lives. If they are to develop a healthy self-confidence, they must encounter an environment that's structured for success.

Without these successes, the child may develop a weak sense of personal identity and worth that can hinder emotional growth. It does not take many early failures for children to see themselves as inadequate—an attitude that's difficult to reverse. In his book, *Teaching the Child Under Six*, James L. Hymes, Jr., says:

"Success matters very much to the under-six group. These children want so desperately to be able to hold their heads high. They sound exceedingly boastful: 'I can count up to five . . . I can tie my shoes . . . .' But we must not be misled by this drum-beating. The bombast is as much for the child's benefit as for ours—he can't quite believe his own importance."

Five-year-olds can't risk failure and should not be compared to one another. It's a good idea to stay away from games, races, and contests with winners and losers. During group discussions, children should never feel they give a "wrong" answer. Any response can be framed with "You are really thinking," or similar positive encouragement. To tell a child "No, that is the wrong answer," gives the child a sense of failure and discourages his future participation. Self-confidence is not built on one or two large successful experiences; it takes many small successful experiences that compound daily.

Your importance in preparing an environment that will encourage and support the child cannot be over-emphasized. Along with the structured environment, you guide all children to a sense of caring for others. Many children will not be able to value or believe in themselves until someone else respects them. A kind, interested teacher believes in each child.

There are many ways of helping all children feel worthwhile. Perhaps one can build a wonderful block structure, or gallop well, or is very good

> *Be positive in your approach to everything you do.*

at helping with clean-up. Supportive attitudes and words tell them that they are important and build confidence and personal satisfaction. They grow in any area which allows them to do things for themselves.

You, as a professional teacher, care about all children and help them build good self-concepts—the right start for both school and life. The following are some simple, but important, techniques for developing self-esteem.

★ Greet each child by name. Make all feel welcome and important.
★ Create an open, caring environment that the child enjoys.
★ Smile. It makes everyone feel better.
★ Be positive in your approach to everything you do.
★ Look directly at the child when talking with him.
★ Listen and respect what the children say.
★ Tell the returning child that you missed him.
★ Encourage and touch all children when appropriate occasions arise.
★ Let the rule-breaker know "I like you, but I don't like what you are doing."
★ Display the children's work.
★ Smile as you tell the children "Goodbye."

The Kindergarten Classroom

Setting the Stage

The Room

Before the children arrive on the first day of school, you can create an inviting environment through your preparation. Make sure that only equipment that will be used is visible—it's very frustrating for young children to see materials that are not available to them.

> *Design your classroom so it has many centers of interest that allow children to learn separately or together.*

Bulletin boards should be simple and attractive. Incorporating the children's names on a bulletin board is a good touch—one possibility is a fall scene with colored leaves falling on the ground and each child's name on a leaf; another is an oak tree with acorns scattered on the ground and names on the acorns. Make sure you have blank leaves or acorns available for children who aren't on the class list.

Name tags for those first days of school are important; you need to be able to call each child by name. Using the same design (leaves or acorns) as used on the bulletin board provides an opportunity for a matching game. Name tags can be pinned on or hung around necks with yarn. Tell the children that caring for their name tag is their "job"; you can decide whether to keep the tags in the classroom or let the children take them home each day.

A decorated bulletin board should also have some blank areas where children's work can be posted after the first day. Some children won't want to leave their work; don't insist if a child *needs* to take his work home. Whenever possible, have a sample of each child's work on display.

A calendar and weather chart should be ready to use the first day if the schedule permits.

Plants add interest and warmth to the room; a hanging basket is attractive. Also have empty vases on hand for children who bring flowers. Different-sized cans, sprayed with bright paint, make attractive containers.

Interest Centers

Design your classroom so it has many centers of interest that allow children to learn separately or together. The centers should be versatile and flexible, so that there are activities and experiences appropriate for each child. This isn't hard to accomplish because children will act on or react to materials and experiences at different levels. One child, for example, is ready to simply string beads; another is ready to put the beads on the string in patterns of color and number; a third is ready to develop reading skills by looking at a pattern printed on a card and replicating it on a string of beads.

Some centers remain in the room all year; others come and go—particularly those related to a current unit of study. The time of the year and the size of the room will determine how much can be out at one time. Make sure there's a large open space in the center of the room for circle games and activities. During worktime, this area can be used for block building.

Here are some suggested centers and related equipment:

Reading center

★ A reading table with books which have been read during story time.
★ A book shelf with additional reading material.

Listening center

Cassette recorder and tapes. There are good commercial book and tape sets, but children most enjoy hearing the teacher's voice, the principal's voice, or a parent's voice.

Math center

★ Counting sticks
★ Flannel board and aids
★ Beads, strings, pegs, and peg boards
★ Cubical counting blocks
★ Clock dial
★ Unit blocks, scales, and measuring tools
★ *Mathematics Their Way* materials, tubs, and games

Manipulative center

★ Kindergarten dominos
★ Picture dominos
★ Lotto games
★ Tinker Toys
★ Puzzles
★ Lincoln Logs
★ Legos
★ Cuisenaire rods

Cooking center

★ Electric roaster
★ Electric skillet
★ Popcorn popper

Make sure there's a large open space in the center of the room for circle games and activities.

- ★ Cooking utensils
- ★ Crockpot
- ★ Kindergarten picture cookbook

Creative center

- ★ Easels
- ★ Crayons
- ★ Crayon melters
- ★ Cheese grater (to shave broken crayons)
- ★ Wallpaper book
- ★ Paste
- ★ Glue
- ★ Finger paints
- ★ Clay
- ★ Cloth scraps
- ★ Scissors

Science center

- ★ Magnet
- ★ Incubator
- ★ Terrarium
- ★ Aquarium
- ★ Rocks
- ★ Plants
- ★ Shells
- ★ Plant cuttings
- ★ Prism
- ★ Ant farm
- ★ Magnifying glass

Writing center

- ★ Old typewriter or computer
- ★ Paper, pencils, and crayons
- ★ Wipe-off cards
- ★ Sandpaper letters
- ★ Magic slate

Music center

- ★ Xylophone
- ★ Autoharp
- ★ Rhythm band instruments
- ★ Record player
- ★ Tape player

Woodworking center

- ★ Workbench
- ★ Nails

★ Vise
★ Sandpaper
★ Wood glue
★ Hammers
★ Soft wood scraps
★ Saws
★ Planes
★ Safety goggles

Grocery store

★ Empty cans and boxes brought from home
★ Cash register with play money
★ Play food

Beauty and barber shop

★ "Hair dryer" (made from a three-gallon round ice cream carton)
★ Combs and brushes
★ Wigs
★ Shaving cream
★ Razors without blades
★ Towels
★ Accessory shop (items donated by parents)
★ Jewelry
★ Scarves
★ Hats
★ Gloves

The Visit before the Year Begins

Some schools have a pre-school visitation day for parents and children to visit the room and meet the teacher. During this visit, parents make an appointment for a pre-school conference.

This is a good time to give name tags to the children. Tell the children it's their "job" to take care of the tag and to remember to wear it each day until you say that they don't have to anymore. The name tag enables you to call the children's names as they enter the room—part of the process of building self-esteem.

A conference with only the parents at the beginning of the year or before school starts is very productive and well worth the effort.

Parent Conferences before School Begins

A conference with only the parents at the beginning of the year or before school starts is very productive and well worth the effort. We think it is so beneficial that it's one of the few things we recommend doing on your own time *if necessary*. It provides an opportunity to learn about each child, but the greatest benefit is getting acquainted with the parents when all is well. If areas of concern arise later in the year, it is much easier to communicate if you and the parents already have a positive relationship.

This conference can start with a simple statement like "Tell me about your child," or "Is there anything you can tell me about your child that will help me at school?" It doesn't have to last long—ten to twenty minutes is usually ample.

The conference is also a good time to find out how the child will go home from school, and for you to emphasize the security a child feels if someone is waiting when school is over. Children want to see a familiar face immediately—if they don't, a fearful attitude toward school may develop. The child's need to be met by someone cannot be overemphasized.

Children listen more attentively if you speak in a low voice.

If there has not been a pre-school visitation, the conference is a good time for you to give the child's name tag to the parents and impress upon them how important it is for the child to wear it on the first day of school.

It's a good idea to end with the statement, "If you ever have a concern, don't hesitate to call, and I will do the same." The parents learn that you want a combined effort from yourself and them to ensure success for the child.

The First Day

Many a new teacher has had laryngitis in the fall because she's assumed she has to address the group loudly and has strained her voice. Actually, children listen more attentively if you speak in a low voice.

The first day should include teaching the children the "Three Rules" song, a fun song that teaches them the kindergarten rules that are the basis for appropriate behavior. You'll find it in the Resource Section.

The first day sets the stage for the entire year. If the teacher is prepared, relaxed, and ready for an exciting year, the children will sense this and respond with similar attitudes.

The following techniques are helpful in establishing and maintaining control of the classroom. Use them at the beginning of the school year and be consistent with their use throughout the year to help teach the children good habits.

The talking instrument. This practice originated when every kindergarten had a piano, but it can be used just as easily with a toy xylophone or autoharp. On the first day of school, as the children enter, take each by the hand and say, "Let me show you where we will sit when we come to school." You show them how to sit in a semi-circle. After all have arrived, strike a few notes on the instrument. This gets their attention long enough for you to say, "Good morning, boys and girls. Did you know I have a talking xylophone? It is a very special xylophone. It talks only to children and only they know what it is saying. Grown-ups cannot hear it like you can." This makes a hit with them. They are already beginning to feel special. You play C, E, and G and explain that the xylophone is saying "Please be quiet." Say you will play it again, and each child who hears what it says should raise his hand. You play C, E, and G. Hands go up! Next, play any note twice, which means "Please stand." You say you will play it again and if they hear it, they should stand. Success again! You explain that there will be a few times when you have something to say and if they are busy, you will play the two notes. Another signal is C, G, E, and C, which says "Please go to work." This is used after all worktime activities have been chosen and everyone can start in the interest centers.

At the beginning of the year, the children will have a short attention span and cannot stay with one activity for very long.

Secret signals are the best way to teach children how to sit during group time. Again, explain that only you and they will know what you mean when you call out a secret signal number. Children seem to derive joy from this bit of private knowledge. Secret signals can be used without fail throughout the year.

Secret signal 1: Legs crossed (so we won't trip our friends).
Secret signal 2: Hands in lap (so no one will step on them).
Secret signal 3: Sit tall and look happy.

You can review the signals during the first few days of school and throughout the year you can correct misplaced or wandering hands merely by saying, "Secret signal 2!" It works and is better than calling someone's name or saying, "OK, let's have everyone's hands in their laps."

The Schedule

The first day of school should have a minimum of distractions and a maximum of teacher/pupil interaction. A graduated schedule is the preferred plan for the first week of school; a sample appears at the end of this section. A graduated schedule starts with a short time at school the first day and lengthens that time every day until the end of the first week, when children stay for the entire time. This approach provides a comfortable transition to school, and parents generally cooperate when they understand its benefits for the child. However, situations vary and if this is not feasible, flexibility in scheduling activities within the school day can be substituted. An alternative to the graduated schedule is also included in this section.

At the beginning of the year, the children will have a short attention span and cannot stay with one activity for very long. Use two short work periods instead of one long period and gradually lengthen the periods until the children are ready for a long one.

Sample Schedule for the First Week of School, Half-Day

(The songs and games referred to can all be found in the Resource Section.)

First Day (8:45 - 10:00 a.m. or 12:45 - 2:00 p.m.)

★ Talking piano and its secret signals.

★ Taking roll (called "name game"). Ask children to raise hand and say, "I am here."

★ Discuss how we can tell who is a kindergartner (he can sit still, listen, not interrupt, and follow directions).

★ Teach a "good morning" song (this is a good way to start the day in a positive way)., Teach "Three Rules" song.

★ "Do as I Do" activity: Teddy Bear; Jumping Jack; Open Them, Shut Them; or any other suitable activity poem.

★ Teach a finger play, do a tiptoe rhythm.

★ Story time.

★ Introduce reading table.

Second day (8:45 - 10:30 a.m. or 12:45 - 2:30 p.m.)

★ Review signals.

★ Sing greeting and "Three Rules" song, teach a flag song, and do name game.

★ Introduce and discuss drinking fountain and bathroom procedures.

★ Have each child get a drink.

★ Introduce coloring, beads, and playhouse. Discuss taking turns and returning materials.

★ Share some of the coloring.

★ Teach a song; do rhythms, tiptoes, walking, hopping.

★ Story time.

Third Day, full session (8:45 - 11:15 a.m. or 12:45 - 3:15 p.m.)

★ Review signals.

★ Sing opening songs (greeting and flag), do name game, and introduce calendar and weather activities.

★ Work with coloring, beads, and introduce pegs, blocks, puzzles, and easel painting.

★ Outside time.

★ Quiet time with music or short story.

★ Music (sing all songs learned) and rhythms.

★ Game (hot ball or bounce ball).

★ Story time.

Alternative to the Graduated Schedule

First day

8:45 - 9:30 a.m. or 12:45 - 1:30 p.m.

★ Teach secret signals.

★ Roll call (name game).
★ Discuss sitting, listening, and following directions.
★ Teach a "good morning" song.
★ Teach "Thumbkin," a tiptoe rhythm.
★ Read a story.
★ Introduce reading table.
9:30 - 10:00 a.m. or 1:30 - 2:00 p.m.
★ Outdoor activity or a walk.
★ Locate bathroom and drinking fountain.
10:00 - 11:15 a.m. or 2:00 - 3:15 p.m.
★ Back in room, explain use of bathroom signal.
★ Review signals.
★ Repeat name game.
★ Teach a flag song.
★ Introduce coloring, beads, pegs, and playhouse.
★ Play a short game.
★ Safety poem.
★ Get ready to go home.

Second Day

8:45 - 9:15 a.m. or 12:45 - 1:15 p.m.
★ Review signals.
★ Sing opening song and rules song, do name game and flag song.
9:15 - 9:45 a.m. or 1:15 - 1:45 p.m.
★ Review bathroom procedure.
★ Explain sharing, taking turns, and how to keep track.
★ Introduce blocks and puzzles.
★ Worktime, beads, coloring, blocks, playhouse and easel painting.
★ Return materials.
★ Show some children's coloring.
9:45 - 10:15 a.m. or 1:45 - 2:15 p.m.
★ Outside activity.
10:15 - 10:25 a.m. or 2:15 - 2:25 p.m.
★ Quiet time.
10:25 - 10:50 a.m. or 2:25 - 2:50 p.m.
★ Teach a song, do some rhythms.
10:50 - 11:15 a.m. or 2:50 - 3:15 p.m.
★ Story time and get ready to go home.

Third day, regular schedule (see page 26)

The Art of Classroom Management

Even the first day, children are entitled to know your expectations. After that, your observation and follow-through are important. This takes a sharp mind and keen eye. The professional makes it look easy; it is not. Your concentration and use of energy can be a drain the first few weeks, but it will pay dividends through the year. Conversely, an undisciplined start will create a lingering uncertainty for the rest of the year. With effective management, each child will derive maximum value from your prepared environment.

By the end of two or three weeks, most students understand what is expected of them and only occasional reminders will be necessary.

Your long-range goal is for the children to develop self-control, but since that's a slow, all-year process, you need techniques to avoid chaos during the beginning weeks of school.

We don't condone the negative approach, with you as the authority figure—demanding certain behaviors "or else"; and "letting them know who is boss." Such practices may mean well but will result in students with robot-like behavior that disappears when the authority is not around. We've heard the "Don't smile until after Christmas" theory, but we don't go along with that, either. A smile is part of the curriculum; it's contagious.

You, as an effective teacher, have to have control even when you're working with the children to help them determine how everyone can get the most out of this new environment—an important adjustment necessary for group activity.

For the first few weeks, you can achieve control by being a performer, keeping the children's attention through various skills such as singing directions, always asking the children for special help, constantly asking them if they remember the "three rules," etc. At the same time, give them small doses of what you expect from them in the way of behavior. By the end of two or three weeks, most students understand what is expected of them and only occasional reminders will be necessary. Your careful work will pay off for the rest of the year—perhaps for the rest of the children's lives.

Quiet Time

Quiet time in the middle of the session has some value but is not very popular with the children. Fives tire easily but they're willing to go until they drop or become irritable. An active, vigorous program can use a quiet time of ten minutes, *no more*, during which the children sit or lie quietly. It also helps to motivate the children to want to rest quietly. Many teachers have crowns made of construction paper for a King and Queen—the best resters of the day. If you do this, keep track so you can pass the honor around. Other teachers simply make the best resters the leaders for the day. Whatever the honor, those chosen are a bit special for the rest of the day: they sit in front at story time, lead the group out when it is time to go home, etc. Quiet music during rest time can also create a more relaxing atmosphere.

Don't impose any form of humiliation such as sitting in a corner or standing in the hall.

Using the Bathroom

Try to create a pattern in which the children use the bathroom during worktime. Exceptions will have to be made, but not very often once the children get the idea. Some children may repeatedly want to use the bathroom at other times; they can be prompted with a suggestion a few minutes before worktime is over. Again, a signal helps.

To help the children know when the bathroom is unoccupied, make a cardboard circle with red on one side and green on the other, and hang it from string or yarn near the entrance to the bathroom. Or, if the child has to leave the room to use the bathroom, put it by the door to the room. It helps if this signal can be seen from any place in the room. When a child has to use the bathroom, he turns the signal red before he goes. When he comes back, he turns the signal to green. The children have seen stop lights and usually know the red means "wait until someone comes back" and green means "you can go now." For reading exposure, you may want to put "stop" on the red side and "go" on the green. You'll need to monitor this procedure closely for the first few weeks; the children may forget to turn the signal. After a while, it's just part of the day.

Using the Drinking Fountain

Undesirable activities can be curtailed if the children are taught to drink with one hand on the faucet and the other behind their backs. While learning so many of your other expectations, they accept this without question.

Disruptive Behavior

Disruption is anything that keeps the other children from having a productive experience.

Some minor corrections can be achieved by praising another child. "I like the way John is sitting" usually motivates everyone else to shape up. The simple statement, "You forgot our rule," before you have a chat with the offender can also be effective. "You forgot" gives the offender a way back.

Remember what we said earlier about children forming lifetime attitudes while very young? Don't impose any form of humiliation such as sitting in a corner or standing in the hall. If a child is truly disruptive, however, something has to be done for the benefit of the rest of the class. Have a "time out" area, possibly with a chair and table, where the offender can read a book, color, or whatever. The child has to stay there until he

> *The only time we have seen "time out" fail is when the teacher is wheedled into giving another chance before the child has to go to the area. If she gives in to "I won't do it anymore," all is lost.*

agrees to follow the rules. He is no longer involved in the activities in the classroom, but the time is still productive for him while the rest of the class is enjoying other activities. It is a good idea to discuss this technique and the "time out" area before it has to be used.

If the child is disruptive while in the "time out" area, or if one child is a repeat offender, seek the cooperation of your principal. We want the children to know the principal as their friend, so we don't send them to the office to be spanked (it still happens). Instead, when a child is sent to the principal's office, a conversation something like this one might take place:

Principal: Why are you here?

Child: I was breaking a rule (we used this procedure and in twelve years, not one child failed to tell us why he had come to the office).

Principal: Where did that get you?

Child: Here.

Principal: Is it as much fun here as it is there?

Child: No.

Principal: Right! But you will have to stay here until you agree to follow the rules.

Staying in the office can be pretty dull, so it won't take long for him to decide to follow the rules. If this doesn't solve the problem, a conference with the parents is in order. Ideally, all will agree that if the child misbehaves after talking with the principal, he will have to go home. Do not surprise parents with this policy; they have to understand and agree with it in advance. Most children feel they are being denied something when they cannot go to kindergarten, and this approach is a humane way of giving them two messages: (1) going to school is a privilege and (2) that there are certain ways one must behave in order to receive that privilege. Some principals have created isolated spots in the office for children who can't be sent home; the child spends the rest of the day in the isolated spot. As long as the child remains in view of adults and has appropriate materials to work with, this is not an abusive approach—just one that few children want to repeat.

The only time we have seen "time out" fail is when the teacher is wheedled into giving another chance before the child has to go to the area. If she gives in to "I won't do it anymore," all is lost. Once a child is told to go to the "time out" area, he must go. After all, how long he stays is up to him.

Coping with Tattlers

The tattletale is not as interested in getting the other child in trouble as he is in letting you know that *he* knows the rule. If you say, "I am so glad you know that rule," he considers the situation handled.

Scheduling

Having a daily schedule makes the children feel more secure and enables the program to operate in an orderly fashion.

The day should be organized around routines while allowing for flexibility. The clock is not sacred. Follow the programmed sequence, but don't pass up the "unexpected" or "special" event.

The focus of the program is on worktime, during which children follow their curiosity into growing knowledge and self-direction. This period should be long enough to allow completion of projects and include time for the task of replacing materials. Cleaning up develops responsibility—don't do anything for the children they can do for themselves.

Large group times are used to plan, to discuss, and to impart information. Songs, games, and storytime are also appropriate activities for large group times.

Small group times are effective for individualization and evaluation, with the teacher serving as a catalyst.

The daily schedule should be prominently displayed. Current lesson plans placed just outside the room are a good way of informing everyone that the day is meticulously planned.

While schedules can differ in many ways, there are some helpful guidelines. Your schedule should have:

★ Periods of time consisting solely of group activities, worktime, music and rhythms, quiet time, and outside time.

★ A balance between active and quiet experiences, and between individual work and large or small groups.

★ Adequate time to prepare to go home.

★ Consistency with flexibility.

Including a specific hour on the schedule is helpful for a substitute or volunteer, but don't be a slave to the clock. As long as the sequence of activity remains the same, the amount of time spent on each can vary.

The sample schedules have proven successful but are only suggestions. You must adjust your schedule (periods of time) to the characteristics of the children.

Follow the programmed sequence, but don't pass up the "unexpected" or "special" event.

Sample Schedules

Half Day

Morning Session	Activities	Afternoon Session
8:45 - 9:00	*Opening Period* Greeting song Flag song Name game Stand-up activity	12:30 - 12:45
9:00 - 9:15	*Calendar and Weather* Our news Introduce new material Discussion of theme and/or science experience or reading or math experience	12:45 - 1:00
9:15 - 9:55	*Worktime* Self-selected activities Return of materials Evaluation	1:00 - 1:40
9:55 - 10:10	*Outside Time* Unstructured	1:40 - 1:55
10:10 - 10:20	*Quiet Time* Story or music	1:55 - 2:05
10:20 - 10:30	*Activity* Reading or math	2:05 - 2:15
10:30 - 10:45	*Music* Singing Rhythms Games	2:15 - 2:30
10:45 - 11:05	*Story Time* Stories Poems Dramatizations	2:30 - 2:50

11:05 - 11:15	*Preparation for Dismissal* Collect work Get wraps Distribute bulletins Goodbye song	2:50 - 3:00

Full Day Schedule

8:45 - 9:30	*Opening Period* Greeting song Flag song Name game Stand-up activity Calendar and weather Our news Introduce new material Discussion of theme and/or reading or math experience
9:30 - 10:30	*Worktime* Self-selected activities Return of materials Evaluation
10:30 - 11:15	*Outside Time* Unstructured
11:15 - 11:30	*Planned Activity* Reading, math, or science experiment
11:30 - 12:00	*Music* Singing Rhythms Games
12:00 - 12:45	*Lunch* Quiet games Reading
12:45 - 1:15	*Quiet Time* Music or story

1:15 - 2:00	*Worktime* Self-selected activities Return of materials Evaluation
2:00 - 2:30	*Outside Time* Unstructured
2:30 - 2:45	*Story Time*
2:45 - 3:00	*Preparation for Dismissal* Collect work Get wraps Distribute bulletins Goodbye song

The End of the School Year

The kindergarten program that continues through the last minute of the last day is a class act. That is as it should be. The professional does not pick up and put away until the last "goodbye." The last weeks of school can be as exciting and productive as the first. Like the first days, the final days require planning and an open mind. (There is a unit theme suggestion in the Resource Section that centers on the last days of school.)

The professional does not pick up and put away until the last "goodbye."

Save something new for the end of the year—a game, a new manipulative, a new puzzle, new story books.

An end-of-the-year conference has as much value as the pre-school conference, especially in its benefits for parents' attitudes toward your school system. The school year is over, and you still care! What a message!

It doesn't take much time to report the child's accomplishments and to thank parents for their help and cooperation. This is also a good time for a word or two about the unrealistic pressures and expectations put upon the first-grade teachers.

Parents appreciate written suggestions for summer activities which are suited for the children. Encourage parents to:

★ Continue to read at least one story a day.

★ Visit the library.

★ Build the children's vocabulary by taking them places.

Then . . .

Have a good summer, and a different next year.

Planning and Using Unit Themes

A classroom of students busily engaged in a variety of activities, moving at their own pace from one area to another, may appear to be a room where children are "turned loose to play." The enlightened teacher knows that wondering, asking, talking, and moving are appropriate ways for learning to take place at the kindergarten level. Such an environment does not happen by accident; it is the result of good creative planning.

The individualized curriculum provides activities that can encompass a wide range of academic levels on different subjects. These choices are available according to the needs of the students; as the year progresses the activities will change. Consequently, planning is necessary to ensure a successful curriculum.

Planning

Many teachers find it helpful to make tentative plans for the calendar year using unit themes, which provide a framework for discussion and concept development. These themes must have relevance for the students. Many are "built in" by the time of year itself, i.e., holidays and seasons; others develop from the interests of the class or individual students or from something such as a parent's occupation. A good teacher recognizes opportunities and plans accordingly.

The individualized curriculum provides activities that can encompass a wide range of academic levels on different subjects.

Establish your general goals for the year, then plan the various unit themes (usually lasting one week) with appropriate activities incorporating specific concepts related to the theme.

Determine what materials and equipment are necessary. These materials should be available to the children once the unit study has begun (for example, resource books, stories, songs, poems, records, tapes, films, etc.).

A culminating activity can be a high point of a unit theme; sometimes the children can be included in the planning of this activity. A field trip, illustrations of an experience, or a special cooking activity are good culminating activities. You can enhance a culminating activity by discussing it with children and asking them to dictate and/or illustrate a story about the experience.

Your written comments on current lesson plans are useful for future planning. Make sure you record the interest level of the children, but remember that each year the children will have different needs and abilities. As new ideas and materials become available, they can be incorporated into a theme.

The room itself has an impact on learning. The room should provide activities that immediately involve the children. A well-planned atmosphere helps a child think, "This is my room and I like being here."

Reinforce the current unit theme by reflecting it in the room—when you're studying outer space, let the children set up the the big block area as a rocket ship.

A well-planned atmosphere helps a child think, "This is my room and I like being here."

An experienced teacher knows that too much planning is far better than having extra time and wondering what to do next. Even transition times, when students are moving from one activity to another, will go more smoothly if the teacher has planned every minute. Good planning provides children with the security derived from a consistent sequence. Good teaching includes the flexibility which leaves room for the unplanned "teachable" moment.

Implementation

At the kindergarten level there are many timeless and universal themes; generally they last about a week but can be extended. Choosing a theme is your prerogative, and although the pages that follow list more themes than can be used within the school year, there are many more that can be added. You will recognize opportunities to develop a theme unique to a particular class or around activities within a community or state. The most important guideline is the theme's relevance to the students.

The introduction of a unit theme is enhanced by pictures, stories, books, and concrete materials which can stimulate interest and encourage discussion. These resource materials should be on the child's level. It can be beneficial for parents to know in advance what is being introduced.

Theme discussion can start at the beginning of the day. Perhaps the interaction begins with a related picture or story. Provocative questions require more than a "yes" or "no" answer. A discussion will usually develop naturally, but it helps to have more props and questions than you might need.

Unit themes often provide ideas for a specific interest, i.e., a "Shopping Center" unit can lead to setting up a department store, or "Postal Workers"—a post office. Interest centers such as these might contain big blocks, cardboard boxes and props. A collection of props, such as a stethoscope for a "Doctor and Nurse" unit, or Indian bead work for an Indian theme, can help develop the unit.

Several related activities can be available for students during self-selection time; most should be optional.

The Resource Section of this book has many suggestions for activities such as crafts related to a unit theme, fingerplays, activity poems and games. You can add your own music, rhythms, stories and poems.

Suggested Themes

We've found the following themes to be useful. There are many more that will fit into the kindergarten curriculum, and you should always be aware of the children's needs and interests when planning. In the Resource Section of this book, the following themes are developed into units which include understandings, worktime, interests, and theme discussion.

The introduction of a unit theme is enhanced by pictures, stories, books, and concrete materials which can stimulate interest and encourage discussion.

LEARNING ABOUT OUR SCHOOL
LEARNING ABOUT OUR KINDERGARTEN
SCHOOL HELPERS
SAFETY
ALL ABOUT ME
NUTRITION
COOKING
THE FAIR
HALLOWEEN
FALL
INDIANS
THANKSGIVING
WINTER
CHRISTMAS AND HANUKKAH
A NEW YEAR AND TIME
TOYS
SNOW
WHERE WE LIVE
HEALTH AND SAFETY AT HOME
POSTMAN
VALENTINE'S DAY
GEORGE WASHINGTON
ABRAHAM LINCOLN
OUR COUNTRY
OUR STATE
EASTER AND SPRING
WINDY WEATHER
SPACE
BIRDS
PETS

SPIDERS AND INSECTS
PLANTS
GARDENING
THE FARM
OUR ENVIRONMENT
SHOPPING CENTER
THE CIRCUS
THE FIREMAN
THE POLICEMAN
DOCTOR AND NURSE
DENTIST
THE ZOO
TRANSPORTATION
EATING OUT
VACATION TIME
GETTING TO KNOW FIRST GRADE

A Day in Kindergarten

Starting the Day

The opening period creates an atmosphere that influences the rest of the day. Use this time as an opportunity to make the children feel welcome, share "news" with them, and stimulate their interest in activities planned for the day.

It takes a few days for the children to learn how to enter the room and sit in a semi-circle. Once that becomes routine, start the day by being seated and ready in your chair at the front of the semi-circle when the children arrive. Some teachers use a small chair, others prefer a rocking chair. When the first child enters, stop whatever you're doing and sit in the chair. Greet each entering child by name. Visit with the children and allow them to visit with each other. Child by child, you are achieving control for the day. The casual visiting continues until it looks like all the children have arrived.

Some teachers establish a signal that means it's time to start the day, such as a bell or a note on the piano or other instrument. Others start singing a "Good Morning" song and the children sing along.

Start the day by being seated and ready in your chair at the front of the semi-circle when the children arrive.

Saluting the Flag

Some programs follow the "Good Morning" song by saluting the flag. We have heard many of the "cute" mistakes children make when saying the pledge, and prefer building respect for the flag in a more age-appropriate way, such as a flag song. We would prefer to see the pledge become a unit of study in third or fourth grade when there can be more understanding. (Homework at the third-grade level could involve finding definitions of the words pledge, allegiance, republic, etc.)

Taking Attendance

Schools need an accurate attendance record, and you must accomplish this without losing control. We have three suggestions.

1. Beginning of the year

Explain your "name game"—that you will call a name and when each child hears his name, he will raise his hand and say, "I am here." This helps children learn each others' names.

2. Second semester (earlier if the class is ready)

Hold up name cards to which each child will respond, "I am here." Hand-raising is no longer necessary. This technique helps the children learn to read each others' names.

3. Later in the year

A pocket chart holds the name cards. As children enter the room, each takes his name card out of the chart and places it at a designated spot. Unclaimed cards reveal who is absent.

Welcoming Absentees Back

Call children returning from absence to stand by you while the class sings a welcoming song such as:

(Tune: "The Farmer in the Dell")

We're glad that you are back,
We're glad that you are back,
Heigh-ho the derry-o,
We're glad you're back today.

When possible, an elementary math experience (set, sub-sets) might follow, with you asking, "How many boys did we welcome back?" You "prove" the answer by touching each head as the children count. Repeat with the girls, and then with boys and girls together.

Calendar activities provide a framework for introducing concepts in addition to numbers and time.

Show and Tell

Children need opportunities to express themselves and gain experience speaking in front of others, but "show and tell" can get out of hand. Many teachers use part of early visiting time for this activity. Anything is acceptable during the first week of school; later, set constructive limits as to what can be brought (science items, materials related to a unit of study, a birthday present). If the experience takes too much time, designate one day a week for bringing things from home.

As the year progresses, children will have enough opportunities to express themselves by discussing what was done at worktime.

The Calendar

Calendar activities provide a framework for introducing concepts in addition to numbers and time. The following pre-reading skills can be developed as part of the calendar experience:

★ Exposure to left to right progression of letters and words;

★ An increased vocabulary—names of days and months, which one, how many, before, after, next year, and number. Calendar activities also offer an opportunity for children to work a "one word" response into a complete sentence. For example, instead of just pointing to "Monday" on the calendar, the child can say, "Today is Monday, the 10th of September, 19__. Tomorrow is Tuesday and yesterday was Sunday."

> *Visual discrimination is developed when the children find a numeral near the calendar and match it with the correct numeral on the calendar.*

★ Familiarity with sounds and numbers—calendar time is an excellent opportunity to take a few minutes to discuss sounds and associate those sounds with other words, e.g. Monday, Mary, mother, milk, etc. Children learn to recognize numerals and understand their placement, e.g. numeral before today, after, below, and above today. They learn to use numbers to express relevant periods of time—how many days in a week, month, and how many days until some special day in the month.
★ Exposure to working with numbers—calendar activities enable children to work on the progression of numbers (adding one more); today is the 6th—one more, or tomorrow, is the 7th. They use ordinal numbers i.e., first, second, etc., in stating the date.

Visual discrimination is developed when the children find a numeral near the calendar and match it with the correct numeral on the calendar. This can extend into worktime. Asking questions such as "How many 3s do you see on the calendar?" is an example of working for visual discrimination.
★ Giving the child a sense of being special—birthdays can extend the calendar activity. Marking a child's birthday helps him learn his birthday and helps him relate more closely to the concepts explained by the calendar. Honoring birthdays gives children a sense of identification—a positive experience.

The child who does the calendar activity usually also reports and records the weather. The children learn to listen to weather reports on TV and radio; discussing the weather provides another opportunity for vocabulary building: predict, forecast, temperature, gusty, blustery, downpour, cloud cover, and jet stream are some of the words heard in weather reports.

Suggested Procedures

Draw a monthly numbered calendar on white paper approximately 18" x 21" and provide appropriate season-related symbols with numerals written on them (in September, for example, fall leaves made from construction paper). A suggested list of symbols appears at the end of this section. Each day, a child selects the correct symbol (these are located close to the calendar) with the correct numeral and attaches it to the matching numeral on the calendar. This can be done with push pins. Mark birthdays with a "birthday sticker." Commercial calendars appropriate for this are available.

Develop questions, games, and conversation to involve the children with the calendar. Providing a variety of activities maintains interest.

Mark the weather by using a wheel with various weather symbols around the outer edge of the circle; a movable arrow fastened in the center

> *When kindergartners are able to express their ideas, their thought processes develop and their self-confidence grows.*

points to the weather. Or you can have a familiar character, like Snoopy, holding a sign with word cards that can be moved. There is a picture clue on the word card—on the corner of "sunny," there's a picture of the sun. Commercial weather charts for young children are also available.

Sample Questions for Discussion

1. How many Mondays in this month? Let's count.
2. How many days of the month have gone by? Let's check. (As you touch each numeral, the class counts with you.)
3. Today is Thursday, the 12th; what was last Thursday's number?
4. How many Fridays in this month?
5. Which days do we not come to school? How many this month?
6. Cover a numeral and ask, "What numeral is missing?"
7. What numeral comes before and after the missing numeral?

Example of a game: *(Tune is "Farmer in the Dell")*

September is the month,
September is the month,
Heigh-ho the derry-o,
September is the month.
Monday is the day,
Monday . . .

Suggested Calendar Symbols

September—School bus, fall leaves
October—Ghosts, owls, jack-o-lanterns
November—Indians, Pilgrims, turkeys, pumpkins
December—Christmas trees, Star of David, bells, menorahs
January—Clocks, snowflakes (if it is snowing)
February—Valentines, patriotic symbols
March—Birds, kites, Easter eggs, chicks
April—Umbrellas, ducks
May—Flowers, butterflies
June—Sun
Commercial symbols are also available.

Discussion

Most of the kindergarten day is "discussion time," but the opening period is an excellent time for planned experiences that stimulate discussion. The kindergarten teacher guides the children's innate curiosity into an adventure in learning. When kindergartners are able to express their ideas, their thought processes develop and their self-confidence grows.

Most teachers find that using a unit theme as a focal point for discussion stimulates the children's interest; the questioning spirit of young children can make discussion a challenging time.

When introducing a new unit theme, you might use books, pictures, and concrete materials to stimulate interest. The use of conversation starters gets a discussion underway naturally and spontaneously. A pattern can be established so that when a new unit theme is introduced, there will be pictures near the calendar relating to that theme. The children will learn to anticipate the coming of a new theme and will pick up clues about the topic even before discussion. If the theme is Thanksgiving, discussion can start with "Tell me about this picture." A response may lead to another question, or you may need to do a bit of prompting with your questions: "Who came to the first Thanksgiving?"; "Are the people dressed differently than we do today?"; or "Why are they celebrating?" The children will have had Thanksgiving experiences that will extend the discussion, but you should have questions prepared in case they are needed. Your questions should require more than a "yes" or "no" answer. For instance: "Why do you think the Indians came to the first Thanksgiving?"; "What did they serve?"; "What do you do to celebrate Thanksgiving?"; "Who do you like to have come and visit you for Thanksgiving?"; "Where do you go if you are not at home?"; or "What do you usually have for dinner on Thanksgiving?" Discussion time also allows you to help the children form accurate impressions of their world.

Discussion is part of a continuous growth process.

Stay aware of the five-year-old's attention span, and be prepared to either draw the unit discussion to a close or extend it, whichever is appropriate at any given time.

The major goal of discussion is to provide information, increase vocabulary and comprehension, and nurture the desire to learn. Discussion is part of a continuous growth process.

Worktime

Theme discussion can lead to concrete experiences at worktime. The Thanksgiving theme is echoed by making Pilgrim hats and bonnets, planning a Thanksgiving meal to have at school, and cooking it.

Worktime is the core of the program because it is during worktime that children learn through exposure to physical objects and their peers. Children can act on materials in a logical manner much sooner than they can verbalize that action (which means the teacher evaluates by observing). Logic of thought has to be built on logic of action.

An appropriate environment for kindergarten children is designed to meet their interests and needs, encouraging action, not submission. It provides an organized freedom to learn and follow rules that are necessary when two or more human beings interact.

> *It's best if children are allowed to choose a worktime activity; the quality of the work is better when they feel like doing it.*

At times, you appear to be playing a passive role; in reality you are alert to the needs of each child, available when problems arise, questioning as a method of problem-solving, and always seeking to prevent feelings of failure and/or humiliation.

A good worktime is neither noisy nor quiet. There is much activity accompanied by talking, laughing, questioning, wondering, hammering, browsing—a busy hum. It is essential for children to be in social situations that enable them to discover that there are ideas, wants, and needs other than—and sometimes different from—their own. Conditions must allow orientation in space plus freedom to talk, act, react, collaborate, and contradict. The atmosphere must be relaxed, as if to say that time is allowed for finding out, trial and error, and repetition of a successful achievement. Worktime furnishes these requisites.

It's best if children are allowed to choose a worktime activity; the quality of the work is better when they feel like doing it. However, they must learn that centers have limits as to how many can participate at one time. In addition, they must learn that they can't repeat an activity if they have had more turns than a peer who also wants a turn. Learning to share and take turns is not easy for the "pre-operational egocentric", but it is a step that Piaget found essential to intellectual progress.

It pays to keep track of turns, at least at the popular centers which can be used by a limited number of children at one time. The teacher may forget; the children will not. A chart listing the interest centers and the children's names is helpful.

We prefer limiting the number of children who can work in the popular centers. It reinforces number concepts and develops self-control. On the other hand, some teachers prefer the High Scope method of not limiting the number of participants for specific centers because they believe that children do their own limiting. Do what works best for you.

Introduction of Worktime Activities

We feel there is a preferred order for introducing worktime activities. At the beginning of the school year, each interest center, along with the activities in that center, should be explained to the children. The number of activities are limited at the beginning of the school year, and materials should not be on display until they are available for use. Taking the time to properly introduce materials will stimulate interest—it's worth the effort.

Here are the values and procedures for a variety of worktime activities.

Crayons

Value: Eye-hand coordination; creative self-expression; small muscle development

Procedure: Place paper and crayons where they are to be for the rest of the

year.
State your expectations:
1. At self-selection time, children who wish to color will stand by the materials.
2. At a signal, they will take materials, go to a table, and color.
3. At clean-up time, crayons will be returned to the original location.
4. Colored paper can be placed on:
   a. the take-home shelf—for children who would like to bring their work home,
   b. the leave shelf—for children who would like to have their work displayed,
   c. the share shelf—for children who want to show their creations to their friends.

The Reading Table

Value: Stimulates interest in reading

Procedure: After you have read a story, walk to the reading table and place the book on it. Tell the children books you have read to them are on the table, and they can look at the books during worktime if they choose.

There is more information about the reading table in the section on reading.

Beads

Value: Eye-hand coordination; color recognition; pattern recognition; counting; pre-math skills of order—which one? how many?

Procedure: Show materials (beads) in their container and a few strings with knots on the end. As you string beads, ask the children to name the bead's color as it is strung. The class can count the beads when the string is full—all the beads; how many red, blue, etc.

Demonstrate how beads are removed from the string, placed in the original container, and returned to a designated spot at clean-up time.

Tell the children books you have read to them are on the table, and they can look at the books during worktime if they choose.

Pegs

Similar to beads.

Clay

Value: Eye-hand coordination; creative self-expression; relieving tensions

Procedure: Start with a clay that does not harden, such as a plasticene. Demonstrate how to make the clay soft and workable by squeezing the clay first in one hand, then the other. Show the materials on which clay work will be done (oil cloth, plastic mats or, preferably, pieces of formica). Show the children where the clay and work mats will be placed. That is where they will find them and return them each day.

For a modeling dough that hardens, make only what you will use in a short period of time. Mix one cup of flour, one-half cup of salt, three

> *In a good set of blocks, all block sizes are multiples of the smallest blocks—a subtle but successful introduction to physically dealing with equations.*

teaspoons of powdered alum, and just enough water for a thick consistency. Food coloring or powdered tempera can be added for color.

Unit Blocks

Value: Muscle development; design; thinking in relationships; problem-solving; decision-making; working with others; cooperation; group decisions; sharing; dramatic play

In a good set of blocks, all block sizes are multiples of the smallest blocks—a subtle but successful introduction to physically dealing with equations.

Procedure: State your expectations:

1. Blocks are to be taken off the block shelf as they are needed.
2. Only a certain number of children can work with blocks at one time (usually four).
3. At clean-up time, blocks are returned to shelf by size. This may be color coded and closely watched during the first few weeks. A block box may be quicker, but putting blocks up by size gives children a valuable experience in mathematical classification. It is worth the extra time.

Large Hollow Blocks

Value and procedure are the same as with unit blocks.

These are usually stored on the floor against a wall—they are too large for any container. These are usually the most popular activity all year, and they are very useful when building interest centers connected with unit discussions. All kindergartens should have them.

Playhouse

Value: Dramatization; role-playing; creative self-expression

Procedure: It's best if the playhouse equipment can be out of the room until it is used. Pots, pans, cooking utensils, and tableware are available the first day of use; "grown up" clothes can be added later.

Discuss the rules about maintenance of the playhouse and how it is to be returned to its original order at clean-up time.

Some years the playhouse loses its appeal as a family center; if that happens, it can become a "pretend corner" and converted into a center that coordinates with a theme. It can be a grocery store, hospital, office, post office, farm, etc.

Puzzles

Value: Visual discrimination; eye-hand coordination; spatial relationships

Procedure: State your expectations:

1. Pieces of the puzzle are removed from the puzzle board one at a time, not dumped.
2. A puzzle is never put back on the shelf without being completed. If someone is having difficulty, just ask for help.

3. Once a puzzle is completed, it can be returned to the rack and another puzzle can be taken.

Simple puzzles with a few pieces are introduced first; as the children become adept at those, add more complex puzzles. Later in the year, the simpler puzzles can be removed.

It helps to have a small tray to hold the pieces when they are removed from the puzzle board. Putting a code number on the backs of the puzzle boards and corresponding pieces is very helpful.

Easels

Value: Experimentation with the media; a feeling of mastery over the media; eye-hand coordination; muscle development; creative self-expression

Procedure: If most of the children have not had experience with painting, introduce only one color. Show the children how to hold the brush "on the fat part" and how to wipe off excess paint. Give each child a chance to hold the brush, wipe off excess paint against the side of the container, and paint one line on the easel paper (this takes time but pays off throughout the year).

It helps to have a small tray to hold the pieces when they are removed from the puzzle board. Putting a code number on the backs of the puzzle boards and corresponding pieces is very helpful.

If most of the class has been to nursery school or had painting experiences at home, start with two colors but have a discussion about what happens when you mix the colors (you might demonstrate).

Soup cans with plastic lids or baby food jars make good paint containers; parents will supply them, and you can throw them away or recycle instead of having to clean them.

You will find additional information and ideas in the art section.

The Sand and Water Table

Value: Total involvement—fascination; mathematical experiences; decision-making

Procedure: State your expectations:

1. Wear an apron.
2. If water is spilled, the children mop it up with a sponge.
3. If sand is spilled, the children clean it up with a broom and dust pan or small vacuum cleaner.
4. The children do *all* the clean up.

If the kindergarten does not have a water table, plastic dish pans are a good substitute. A water table provides room for several children to work together. At first, let the children have at it their own way. Later, set up some "problems" i.e. "How many of these (1/4 cup) does it take to fill this (1 cup)?"

Additional materials for the water/sand table include rice (which can be dyed with food coloring) and styrofoam "peanuts." Accessories include measuring cups and spoons, soap suds, an egg beater, boats and ships, plastic fish, and large spoons. Animals, farm implements, cars, and other wheel items work well in sand.

Clean-up Time

This is another area where an initial investment at the beginning of the year pays off. Every time a new center or material for that center is introduced, be sure to tell the children where the materials will be stored, then *emphasize* the importance of returning materials to that same location at clean-up time. At first, you'll need to carefully observe the children as they put things away. Allow no discrepancies, and eventually doing things the correct way will become a habit.

Put the responsibility where it belongs—on the children—and you are helping them to develop good work habits.

Outdoor Play

Outdoor play has always been a part of the kindergarten day, but changes in our culture have made it even more important than it was in the past. If your classroom has a door leading outside, you have an ideal situation; a room located near an entrance to the building is second-best.

> *Put the responsibility where it belongs—on the children—and you are helping them to develop good work habits.*

The opportunity for spontaneous play is less common than it used to be. Children do not leave the house and find someone to play with as easily as we could. Many new communities do not have sidewalks, so children have few areas where they can safely roller skate or ride bikes and scooters. In his book, *The Slow Learner in the Classroom,* Newell Kephart describes his substantial research regarding difficulties with reading. He maintains that children need experiences such as roller skating and bike riding in which maintaining balance involves eyes crossing the median line, because these activities promote eyes working together, as they must in reading. Kephart believes dyslexia can result from the lack of such pre-reading activities. Add his theories to our generalization that, with few exceptions, children do not read until their bodies are well-coordinated, and you have great justification for encouraging the gross motor activities involved in outdoor play.

Outdoor play at school involves getting along with others, decision-making, and problem-solving—just like indoor worktime.

Your responsibilities during outdoor play are similar to your responsibilities during worktime—walking here and there, questioning, suggesting, and evaluating.

During good weather, water play can be moved outside. Children can even "paint" the building with water; they love to do that.

Traditional playgrounds—with swings, a slide, and sometimes climbing bars—don't offer as much learning and motivation as they might. You can supplement a traditional playground with the following:

A large sandbox can be very attractive when outlined with railroad ties. "Large" means several children can choose to be involved in sand play at once. Accessories include pots and pans, measuring cups and spoons, plastic bottles, buckets, spoons, strainers, Jello molds, and small wheeled toys.

Concrete trails (a one-time investment) for trikes, bikes, and wagons (it pays to buy the best).

Balls, large and small.

Balance beams or something similar.

Climbing equipment: a jungle gym, ladders, and cleated board.

Boxes, preferably wooden, but cardboard is better than nothing.

Outdoor play at school involves getting along with others, decision-making, and problem-solving—just like indoor worktime.

Encourage the children to make full use of the playground for:

Motor activities. Running, walking, rolling down hills, balancing, climbing, swinging, pushing, pulling, bouncing or throwing balls, jumping, and climbing.

Creative activities. Water, sand, caring for caged animals, gardening, and woodworking.

Pretending. A stage, cardboard boxes, boats, a small donated car (windows removed), a donated motorcycle (made stationary), and play houses.

Remember the following when planning the ideal playground:

Good drainage. This is essential if a playground is to be of maximum use; regrade yours if necessary.

Variations in the terrain. A hill can be a major asset in creative play. Hills can be created with a few loads of dirt (a piece of sewer pipe under the hill creates a tunnel).

Trails for wheel toys. These can range from a figure-eight to bridges and tunnels, if the budget allows. "One way," "Slow, children playing," and "Stop" signs can be used and moved about to create a change in patterns. Dramatic play can be enhanced by a traffic cop—a policeman who gives tickets for speeding or running a stop sign (Will you have to move inside for a day in court?).

Shade. This is especially important in hot climates. If shade isn't provided by the natural environment, lath structures, raised platforms, and arbors will help.

Storage. Durable trikes and bikes are an investment to be protected. A shed for storage (4' x 4' x 10') which locks will pay for itself.

Everything should be in full view of adults.

On rare occasions, the ideal play area can be built all at once, perhaps along with a new building. If you need a long-range plan, be optimistic; it will happen sooner than you think. We have seen many fathers who are willing to spend weekends building a community facility that will last for years.

Art Activities

> *All children have creative potential when appropriate experiences, opportunities, and materials are provided.*

There is a difference between crafts and art work. Some children may not feel comfortable with free expression in the art media but may find satisfaction through the planned use of craft materials. These activities can help them develop the confidence they need to explore on their own.

In craft work, each child can make something similar—Jack o' lanterns, Indian head bands, etc. Crafts should be optional, as some little hands will not be ready for cutting and other small muscle activities involved.

Art is creative self-expression and the product is unique—the child's very own. The child who has been allowed to talk, investigate, and produce will often proceed to this higher level of revealing his interpretation of his world.

All children have creative potential when appropriate experiences, opportunities, and materials are provided. If you are careful about "teaching" art, the potential will be realized. Your responsibility is to show the children how to use and care for the media, then stand back and let them have at it.

The first accomplishment for children is mastery of the media. Wielding the paint brush, having the crayon go where *you* want it to be is power! It is control! It is mastery!

Mastery is important to the beginning artist, which is why you might see a painting of something recognizable and a few minutes later see the whole sheet painted over. The power over the brush was the fun. Painting the whole sheet, like scribbling with a crayon, is a stage and should not be demeaned. "That was fun, wasn't it?" will result in a positive response. It is the experience, not the product, that has value.

Once satisfied with this new power, children will start expressing what they feel and know. Their stages of development will determine what they want to paint.

Children are not necessarily realistic. The purple cow is fine with the five-year-old. If they fantasize such things, fine. Remember that fantasy is the root of abstract thought, and we don't want to turn that off. If the child who paints a purple cow isn't fantasizing, he may be revealing a sense of humor.

Proportion may not only be unrealistic; it may also be revealing. What children portray as largest is most important to them. In their egocentricity, they may depict themselves as larger than a house.

They know what they have expressed, and they expect you to know, too. Don't allow them to underestimate your intelligence by saying, "What is it?" They'll like it better if you say, "Tell me about it." They'll tell you.

Encouraging Young Artists

Mastering the media is of prime importance; scribbling is a beginning stage in crayon work. Scribbling should never be maligned by adults; parents may have to be advised in this respect. If you refer to scribbling as a design, the children probably will, too. At this stage, it's the process, not the product, that's important. Sometimes adults, hoping to help the scribblers, teach them how to draw something, usually a house. They *eventually* learn that this was a mistake, because children who are taught to color something specific get stuck on that one subject and do it over and over, not progressing to anything else for some time. Teaching how to paint or draw something can atrophy a concept, at least for a while, because it gives children the idea that what they do on their own is not good enough. Supplying materials and patiently encouraging self-expression will produce results that are occasionally far beyond our expectations.

Notice the children whose drawings are very tiny. They are telling you something. These children may be overplaced, painfully shy, or under some sort of stress and/or pressure. Their art work, accompanied by praise and attention, can help free them of whatever tensions they might have and start them on the road to self-assurance.

Never force children to discuss their work with the class. When they are willing, discussing work will help poise and confidence.

Total acceptance and understanding of what the children have done on their own is a fabulous way to provide inspiration for additional creativity.

Do not use adult standards to judge the work. Honor it all. Display it all. You will be rewarded by the wonderful things you witness by the end of the year.

Never force children to discuss their work with the class. When they are willing, discussing work will help poise and confidence.

Writing

Formal writing instruction (practicing how to make letters, staying in the lines, copying something) is not consonant with our philosophy, that "when they can, they will," but all children profit from vicarious writing experiences. They learn from watching you write and most will soon recognize that a sentence starts with a capital letter and has spaces between words.

Few children will say they can read; most will say they can write. They will scribble and draw, but they think they are writing—and they'll tell you what they've written if you ask!

Children do not ask to be taught to read their names; they ask how to write their names. When they learn to write their names, they can read them. That alone is a big clue that writing and reading instruction work better when not separated.

The Whole Language Approach

Using the "whole language" approach is putting the publishers' compartmentalized series to rest. (Hooray!) And kindergarten can be an early phase of the whole language experience.

> *Never correct invented spelling or teach a misspelled word. We have seen children who have been taught phonetic spelling; too many have difficulty making the transition to correct spelling.*

Although whole language instruction is regarded as comparatively new, many early childhood educators have used similar processes for years. Their methods have been derived to some extent from Sylvia Ashton Warner's books, but mostly from Roach Van Allen's "Language Experience" approach. Van Allen's methodology is structured so that children find out:

What I think, I can say.

What I say can be written (by me or someone else).

I can learn to read some of what I dictate.

What I write, I can read.

I see the same letters used over and over.

Each letter stands for one or more sounds that I make when I talk.

In kindergarten, dictation starts with art work. You ask the artist to tell you about his creation. Ask if he wants to write something he has to say about his picture; if he does, write *exactly* what the child says, even if it's not correct by adult standards.

The evolution of dictation usually follows this sequence:

1. The children trace over what you have written.
2. You leave a space for the children to copy below.
3. You write on another piece of paper and the children transfer the text to their coloring or painting.

When you write dictation, say each word as you write it, then point to each word and say it. Next, you ask the child to say it with you.

Some children will decide to write on their own instead of giving you dictation. They use invented spelling (which researchers have found also develops in stages) and write from what they hear. At first they use initial consonants only. Next come the long vowels. When using short vowels they use "e" for "i" and "a" for short "e." As an example, the spelling of grass might start out as "G", then progress to "GS, then "GRS", "GRES", "GRAS", and finally "GRASS."

Never correct invented spelling or teach a misspelled word. We have seen children who have been taught phonetic spelling; too many have difficulty making the transition to correct spelling.

A more recent innovation in emerging literacy does not include taking dictation from individuals. Instead, dictation is taken from groups and the children "write" on their own. The dictation can be in the form of—

★ "Our News" as described in the reading section (below)
★ A "thank you" note
★ An invitation to visit school
★ A "get well" card to a sick classmate

The group dictation allows children to see the reasons for writing. Usually, the children are given something like a spiral notebook or told where paper is available if they want to write. We have learned that children do not say they cannot write. If they scribble (a developmental stage in writing), they will tell you what it says.

With this process, when a child asks you how to write a word, say "Write it the way it sounds to you." You'll witness the onset of invented spelling.

The bibliography lists many fine resources for creative writing. A favorite of many teachers is *Writing: Teachers and Children at Work* by Donald Graves.

We suggest you consider both methods and try the one that seems most comfortable for you and most adaptable for your class. The beautiful aspect of both methods is that there does not have to be any grouping or labeling because both approaches, when used correctly, are self-pacing and success-oriented.

Everything you teach is a stage of reading instruction. Appropriate methods turn children on to reading; inappropriate methods—those more suited to older children—turn the young child off, sometimes permanently.

In either case, the introduction of anything parents might not understand calls for a meeting and/or a bulletin to parents to help them understand why invented spelling is not corrected, and how children emerge from the relevant things they write to reading what they write and eventually to reading what others write.

We emphasize that none of this replaces other tools for small muscle development—beads, pegs, clay, crayons, legos, and other manipulatives.

Writing is encouraged when children are surrounded by print, read to a lot, and given experiences via films, field trips, and visitors in the classroom.

Reading

When asked if you teach reading, your response should never be "No." Nor should it be, "I teach readiness." Your answer should be, "Yes—in ways tailored to how five-year-olds learn."

Everything you teach is a stage of reading instruction. Appropriate methods turn children on to reading; inappropriate methods—those more suited to older children—turn the young child off, sometimes permanently.

We must all work harder to educate parents, administrators, and the entire community about the proper ways to teach reading to five-year-olds. We must stress that children need to be given what they are ready to use.

> *Our goal is to produce children who enjoy reading for information and pleasure.*

We can no longer say formal instruction is wrong without delineating what is right.

Children want to read. When they are ready for the printed word, there is no stopping them. Until that moment, there is plenty we can do.

Expose the children to everything, but pressure them into nothing! It is our belief that there are two kinds of adult non-readers—those who cannot read and those who can read but read only what is necessary. We believe that with few exceptions, non-readers are people who were forced into reading instruction before they were ready.

Our goal is to produce children who enjoy reading for information and pleasure. We want them to become adults who will read for information and pick up a book in their leisure time.

Children entering kindergarten are more diverse in background experiences than ever before. The same class might include some children who have heard little language, and others who have extensive vocabularies and talk constantly. Some may never have heard a story; others have heard a bedtime story every night for as long as they can remember. This diversity alone mandates individualized instruction and is reason enough to rule out any set program or rigid expectations. If children have missed experiences requisite for reading, *the gap must be filled, not skipped.* We and our supervisors have to realize *it takes time to fill gaps.*

There are a few children who can read when they arrive in kindergarten. Over the years we have made inquiries about these children and have been able to arrive at some generalizations:

★ The adults in the home read newspapers, books, and magazines.
★ Stories were read to the children from approximately eighteen months of age.
★ The children did not watch much television, but they stopped playing to watch the commercials.
★ The first words the children read were road signs, logos, etc.

From our investigation, we have deduced that those children watched commercials to learn how to read the product being advertised (most commercials show and repeat the name of the product three times). When they went on errands with their parents, especially to the grocery store, they could read and say the words they had seen on television. How did they teach themselves to read? The "look-say" method! Couple this with Piaget's findings that children are not logical thinkers until approximately seven years of age, and it makes sense to use "look-say" until children are logical, then use formal instruction at about the age of seven. The controversy has always seemed to be "either-or"; it seems more feasible that there is a time and place for each method.

There are many methods which have value on several levels; that is, children will profit from the experiences at different levels of sophistication.

The Exposure Method

The exposure method can be defined as having materials experienced and/or in view. When children are ready to learn the concept or word, it's there. For example, if you start taking attendance with name cards, most of the children will learn to read all of the names but at different times (we call this individualized learning).

Another successful exposure to words is to use labels around the room—"table" on the table, "chair" on the chair. Many items in the room can have label cards attached, and children make the connection—some sooner, some later.

Field Trips

Field trips take quite a bit of planning but are worth the effort. In many ways, we consider field trips the top-notch way to make reading easy for children. Children can sound out "gro-cer-y st-ore" but if they haven't been in one, it doesn't make much sense to read about one.

Some classes may not be ready for field trips until the second half of the year, but a well-planned field trip is a great vocabulary builder and can be the basis for an experience chart (described below) following the trip. No other experience makes such a contribution to cognitive growth, language development, creativity, and new understandings.

For all of the above to be accomplished, you'll need to:

1. Familiarize yourself with the interests of the children and plan accordingly.
2. Visit the area in advance.
3. Secure approval for the visit from the person in charge of the place you want to visit.
4. Make a note of the things you want children to notice, not only at your destination but also on the way there and back. Discuss these with the children before going on the trip.
5. If the library has an informative book about the place you intend to visit, read it to the children the day before the trip.
6. Try to make the visit appropriately paced, so the children are never rushed while they are interested or curious.
7. Plan a follow-up experience. Discuss the trip when you return or the next day. The children can paint and color what they say and dictate an experience chart.

Many items in the room can have label cards attached, and children make the connection—some sooner, some later.

Possible Field Trips

★ A visit to the principal's office.

★ A visit to the custodian to see how the school is heated, cooled, etc.
★ A walk around the school yard—you might choose one tree and observe how it changes with the seasons.
★ Businesses—a shopping mall, all kinds of stores, the airport, the bus station, a bank, a garden, a restaurant, a parent's office.
★ Community facilities—the library, the fire station, the police station, the post office.

Your own situation will give you other ideas.

The Experience Chart

When the children have had an experience such as a field trip, they can dictate a few sentences about what they saw and heard. You can write it on the chalkboard or a chart tablet. The relevance of the situation enables some of the children to start reading the words; those not ready to read the words profit from hearing the words, seeing them written and rethinking the experience.

If children do not want you to "write the story," drop it—they are not ready.

Dictation

This can be a follow-up procedure—much the same as the experience chart —but the children are more involved. If the children choose to color or paint a picture about what they saw on a field trip, they might enjoy dictating a sentence or two about the picture. Of course, this procedure does not have to be limited to field trips. It can be used with any coloring or painting done by the children. If children do not want you to "write the story," drop it—they are not ready. After many dictations about their coloring, some children like to:

1. Trace over the writing with another color crayon;
2. Write below what you have written; and
3. Copy what you wrote on another piece of paper.

If the child is ready for this, fine. If not, fine. Never require this procedure of the class as a whole.

The Daily News

The news can be started during the first week of school. It is the ultimate in the exposure method. News is best done at a chalk board but it can be done at an easel with chart paper.

Explain to the class that mother and father have a newspaper they can read, and from now on we will write our own news at school. Explain that today, and today only, you will decide what the news will be. The news can be something simple like "It is raining outside"; you write the word "It" on the chalk board. Explain that when you start the news you will do it with a big letter (later you can use capital or upper case, but don't actually define the terms. Children pick terms up by connecting what you say with what you do). After writing "It," say "I have finished that word and I don't want it to bump into the next one. What can I do?" Someone will come through with "Leave a little room" or a similar suggestion. You write "is" and ask the same question about bumping words. This time, many give the answer. If you reach the end of the chalkboard, explain that you will go back to continue the story. When you have finished the story or a sentence, tell them the little dot means that part is finished.

The children are not told but are exposed to the fact that you start sentences with capital letters, leave spaces between words, write from left to right, and finish a sentence with a period.

The next day, ask if anyone has news. The responses will be a little more interesting and better every day. "John lost a tooth." "Samantha has a little sister. Her name is Grace." "Jim's daddy got a ticket on the way to school."

After writing the news, read what you have written, touching each word as you read. Then ask the class to read it with you.

If you are fortunate enough to have an aide, she can write some of the words on pieces of paper and the children can find the words after the news has been written. Matching the words can also be a worktime activity.

The daily news is relevant, interesting, and meaningful to the children. Do not be surprised if this is the first thing some of the children read.

Reading stories can be a good way to provide a quiet time for children and calm them down after vigorous activity.

Reading Stories

You can't read too many stories. Children love to be read to, particularly books with action and a good plot. Reading stories can be a good way to provide a quiet time for children and calm them down after vigorous activity. Work in as many stories as you can. The values are endless.

A good story book has illustrations that tell the same story as the words; there are many good inexpensive books on the market. When you read a story, hold the book so the children can see the pictures while you read. As the year progresses, you can ask the children to look at the pictures and tell you the story. Choral response in this case is fine.

After reading the book, put it on the reading table—one of the self-selected activities available during worktime. When a child is looking at a book, you, the aide, or a visiting parent can ask if she would like to hear it again. Later, the child can be asked to read the pictures and tell the story. Some children who frequent the reading table will one day come to you and ask, "What's this word?" Simply answer the question, but realize you have a reader on your hands. In about two weeks that child will be reading his favorite stories. Great, (and reason for a "good news" note to the parents) if the child accomplishes this feat on her own, but *do not make a big deal of it to the class.* There are going to be many children not reading at the end of the year, and that's perfectly all right. Don't make them feel the readers are more special than they are. Their time will come.

Listening Centers

A tape recorder, a recorded story, and a book are all you need to establish a listening center, discussed on page 15.

Mathematics

"Mathematics—the group of sciences (including arithmetic, geometry, algebra, calculus, etc.) that deal with quantities, magnitudes, and forms and their relationships, attributes, etc., by the use of numbers and symbols"

— *Webster*

Relationships, magnitudes, and attributes are pretty high forms of thought, but kindergarten can furnish a broad foundation for mathematics by helping certain children acquire concepts with understanding. Ordinary, everyday experiences can contribute to a strong mathematical background. Although the children might be engrossed in construction, anyone who has to find two small blocks which equal one large block is concretely working with and discovering equations. Additional meaningful activities include counting places in the playhouse, developing one-to-one relationships when placing silverware, counting children for games, and using counting sticks and the flannel board.

It must be emphasized that "counting" refers to the concrete experience of counting objects, not rote recitation. Rote recitation is not proof of understanding; it is frequently just the opposite. An acquired "ability" is meaningless if not accompanied by understanding.

Ordinary, everyday experiences can contribute to a strong mathematical background.

All concepts are achieved via "hands-on" activities with three-dimensional materials. A child who understands the representation of numerals through ten has the foundation for the decimal system. It takes only a few minutes a day, every day, to develop this firm foundation.

There are many fine materials on the market that can help in this regard, and even a small budget can handle the minimum materials necessary for teaching number concepts. This can be accomplished with beads, counting sticks, a flannel board, and flannel cut-outs.

Using Beads

1. Touch and count how many beads are on the string.

2. Touch and count the red beads.
3. Touch and count the blue beads.
4. Draw pictures (there are also commercial cards available) of bead patterns. Have the children put the pattern on the string (one blue, two reds, four green, etc.).

Using Flannel Boards

1. Use flannel cut-outs to make different sized sets of similar objects, (three ducks, five rabbits, etc.)
2. Have children tell how many are in a set; prove it by touching and counting each piece in the set. Later, have the children match a numeral to a set, or give a child a numeral and tell her to find the set with that many objects in it.

Flannel cut-outs can be used to make a set, add to it, take away from it, and count again to see how many are in the set after the changes.

There are all kinds of possibilities for use of the flannel board. Ordinals can be taught by having one cut-out backwards or upside down and asking "Which one is different?"

Concepts for biggest, smallest, more, less, how many, and which one can all be taught with the cut-outs.

Using Counting Sticks (popsicle sticks, toothpicks, etc.)

Have the children sit in a semi-circle on the floor so you can see what everyone is doing.

1. Give each child some sticks. Tell the children to put down one stick.
2. Tell them to put down two more. Ask, "Now how many sticks are on the floor?" Have children touch each stick as they count.
3. Have them pick up one stick and again ask, "How many?"

Working with sticks a few minutes a day (using all kinds of combinations up to ten) is a productive way to instill concepts of the decimal system.

Children are fascinated with counting sticks and like to build and/or make designs with them. After instruction, allow some time for free experimentation with the sticks.

For more information about ways to teach kindergartners about counting, patterning, sorting and classifying, and comparing, we could neither equal nor excel Mary Baretta-Lorton's excellent resource book, *Mathematics Their Way.* This idea-packed book is available from Programs for Education, P.O. Box 167, Rosemont, N.J. 08556.

Children are fascinated with counting sticks and like to build and/or make designs with them. After instruction, allow some time for free experimentation with the sticks.

Science

Science in kindergarten includes observation, questioning, and experimentation, all of which lead to concept development. Be aware of the many opportunities for incorporating scientific discovery, such as using the objects that children bring for sharing. Occasionally, these offerings can lead to building a unit of study. Work to establish a pattern of questioning, observing, and experimenting. When you are consistent in this method and encourage questions, the children will soon be asking "What will happen if . . .?" Remember the importance of interaction with the children (active participants) as opposed to the children always listening (passive participants).

Science experiments should incorporate a control factor when possible. Jell-O is a good basis for a simple experiment. Make Jell-O with hot water, then with cold water, and observe the results. Try using less water and observe the finished product (this "experiment," cut into one-inch cubes, becomes a different type of building block to use during worktime). Taste the three variations and ask for responses.

Science in kindergarten includes observation, questioning, and experimentation, all of which lead to concept development.

The Science Interest Center

The science interest center should have "hands-on" activities which may have evolved out of an experiment and/or interest; these can be self-directed activities (classifying rocks and shells, seeing which items will and will not attract a magnet, seeing which items will and will not float in a pan of water).

There might be permanent objects in the center, such as an aquarium, a magnifying glass with objects to inspect, or caged pets. Science books should be available; relevant pictures will add interest.

A group "story" about an interesting item someone brought to share can be placed in the science center:

Michael brought many shells.
He gathered them at the sea shore.
They are different shapes.

Experiments involving the five senses are easily incorporated into the science curriculum. Along with the five senses, the following themes work well in a science center:

Rocks	Dinosaurs	Ecology
Shells	Birds	Seeds
Sea World	Insects	Plants
Nutrition	Butterflies	Magnets

> *When the children no longer seem interested in the center, change the materials in it. Even within a specific theme, it's best to rotate materials rather than putting everything out at the beginning.*

The science center should be located close to a window to accommodate plants and growing experiments conducted during the year. The children should be responsible for taking care of the different items on display.

When the children no longer seem interested in the center, change the materials in it. Even within a specific theme, it's best to rotate materials rather than putting everything out at the beginning.

Science opportunities are everywhere, and you can integrate science into the curriculum in a variety of ways. Some teachers choose to develop full units that are part of the annual curriculum; others choose to plan one specific day each week for a science experience. Some use a combination of the two methods.

At the kindergarten level, many science activities emerge from the interests of the children and you will enjoy recognizing that "special moment" when an interest can be extended into a meaningful learning experience.

We do want to mention one excellent commercial program. Science Curriculum Improvement Study (SCIS) was developed for kindergarten through sixth grade; the kindergarten level, titled *Beginnings*, is a hands-on, open-ended program. SCIS is published by Delta Education, Nashua, N. H. 03060.

Here are numerous science activities that require only simple, locally available materials.

Suggested Science Activities

Question	Experiment or Observation	Materials
How do trees change during the year?	Choose a tree and take the class to observe it during Fall, Winter, and Spring.	
How do leaves differ?	Place a box of different leaves in the science interest center.	Leaves
What do plants need in order to grow?	Start two sweet potato plants in water. Give one both sun and water. Deprive the other of sun *or* water.	One sweet potato cut in half. Shallow bowl of water.

What fruits have seeds?	Ask children to name some fruits that have seeds. Cut some fruits and observe seeds; e.g., orange, apple, peach, bell pepper. Notice pattern and number of seeds.	Fruits and knife.
How do plants start?	Observe different ways plants start; cuttings, seeds, vegetable tops, and bulbs.	Philodendron cutting, seeds, carrot or beet top, and bulbs.
The Five Senses	Discuss the senses: smell, taste, feel, hear, and see. Make popcorn and have children listen for the popping, smell, taste, feel and see the difference before and after popping.	Popcorn, popper, oil and salt.
The Feel Box. What is in it and how does it feel?	Place objects in a shoe box. Blindfold children and let them take something out, guess what it is, and tell how it feels—soft, rough, smooth, etc.	Shoe box or bag. Objects from room or home: rock, ball, triangle, cotton, sponge, block, etc.
How many different sounds can you hear?	Blindfold children or have them stand where they cannot see but can hear. Make sounds, e.g., triangle, ball bouncing, stamping feet, dropping a book, etc.	Triangle, ball, book, etc.
What do you smell?	Place different items in	Containers and

	containers that children cannot see through, e. g., jars that have been painted but have holes in the lid. Ask children to identify what they smell.	items to smell: lemon juice, cocoa, pepper, cinnamon, etc.
Do things taste different?	Have children taste different items and describe what they taste, e.g., sweet, sour, hot, cool, good, bad, texture, etc.	Different items to taste: dill pickle, sugar, peanut butter, shredded wheat
Is air all around us?	Give children balloons. Have them blow them up. Discuss what is inside.	Balloons
	Make parachutes of varying sizes but put equal weights at the bottom. Discuss why they fall at different speeds.	Different size squares of cloth, objects that weigh the same, and string
Does fire need air to burn?	Light a candle and place it on a saucer. Cover it with a jar. Observe how the flame goes out when all the oxygen is burned up.	Candle, saucer, jar and matches.
Does heat change things?	Make Jell-O as directed. Make using cold water.	Jell-O, cold and hot water.
	Observe popcorn before and after it's popped.	Popcorn, popper, oil, and salt.

What is ice?	Put ice cube in a spoon and hold it over a candle. Observe the results.	Ice cube, spoon, candle, matches
What makes water evaporate?	Wet two cloths. Place one in the sun and other in the shade. Which dries first?	Two cloths
	Place same amount of water in a jar and a pie pan. Observe rate of evaporation. Discuss.	Water jar and pie pan
What can we discover about magnets?	Hold a magnet over different objects. Discuss which ones are picked up and which ones are not. Read *Mickey's Magnet*.	Magnet and several items: paper, pin, clip, penny, pencil, plastic bottle, etc.
When things fall, do they go up or down?	Have children throw different objects up in the air. What happens? Have children jump high. Can they stay up? Discuss. Use globe to explain that although the earth is round, gravity holds us down.	Globe
Are rocks all the same?	Look at a variety of rocks. Break some apart with a hammer. Observe differences between inside and outside. Rub two pieces of sandstone together; do the same with a different rock. Observe differences.	Variety of rocks, including sandstone.

How are tadpoles born?	Find tadpole eggs during spring in a pond. Place in jar or aquarium (without fish) using the pond water. Observe.	Jar or aquarium, eggs, pond water

Music and Rhythm

The primary purpose of music in kindergarten is to expose all children to enjoyable musical experiences, but it serves many other purposes as well. Singing and rhythmic activities are natural forms of self-expression but they can also be cooperative activities. Music time can provide emotional relaxation and is most effective when scheduled near the middle of the day. Songs can expand the children's vocabulary and help improve speech and diction. Language is enriched when you take time to make certain that the children have a meaningful understanding of the words they sing.

Group singing is an activity which provides inner satisfaction through identification with a group. It is an opportunity for the shy child to feel comfortable while participating.

Children learn rhythm, pitch, and tempo while having an enjoyable experience that contributes to lengthening their attention span.

Even though it is planned for a specific time in the schedule, music can flow through the whole day; it can be both planned and spontaneous.

Choosing Music

Songs can be used to complement unit themes, but a song should not be used simply because it fits into a plan. Children particularly enjoy songs that relate to themselves, school, their families, animals, friends, and holidays.

There are several factors to consider when selecting songs: a good melody, rhythmical movement, repetitive phrases, well-written lyrics, appropriate length, voice range, and enjoyment.

Children enjoy:

Nursery rhyme songs	Familiar and unfamiliar songs
Folk songs	Action songs and fingerplays
Fun and nonsense songs	Popular songs

Early in the school year, familiar nursery rhymes set to music are good choices; new songs should be short with repetitive lyrics. As the year progresses, the children will build a repertoire of favorites. It helps to keep a list of songs (and their source) the children have learned. If a song is taught but not enjoyed, drop it.

Group singing is an activity which provides inner satisfaction through identification with a group. It is an opportunity for the shy child to feel comfortable while participating.

> *Some classrooms may not have a piano, or the teacher may not know how to play the piano. This shouldn't stop your class from experiencing music.*

Teaching A Song

You can teach a new song each day; reserve one day each week for "choice day" when the children make the selections.

Ask the children to sit in a group (usually on the floor and near the piano), positioned so you have eye contact with the children. The atmosphere should imply that music is fun.

The following steps help in teaching a new song:

1. Know the song well enough so you can look at the children, not read the lyrics.
2. Introduce the song. Use a picture that relates to the song (many kindergarten song books are illustrated), ask questions about how picture relates to the song, or use a puppet or other object when appropriate.
3. Play the song while the children listen.
4. Sing the song for the children.
5. Say the words and ask the children to say them after you.
6. Play the melody line with one hand and have the children sing.
7. Sing the song together with full piano accompaniment.

This is just one approach to teaching songs; you may develop various effective techniques. The objective is to enjoy music together.

Alternatives to the Piano

Some classrooms may not have a piano, or the teacher may not know how to play the piano. This shouldn't stop your class from experiencing music. Many teachers play instruments that accommodate music in the classroom very well; the guitar, autoharp, and electric keyboard are all good choices. If those aren't viable options, there are many records of songs for early childhood. There is no reason to exclude music from the curriculum.

Listening to Music

Listening to music shouldn't be an isolated or formal situation. Appropriate music can be part of the environment during other activities. Quiet time provides an excellent opportunity for group listening; music helps set the mood for relaxation. Soothing music is appropriate before school and during worktime.

Music appreciation develops through familiarity, and auditory discrimination improves through listening to music; the children will hear high and low sounds, loud and soft sounds, fast and slow rhythms. Listening is a more meaningful experience when the five-year-old learns to listen for definite things and make observations about them.

By exposing the children to music, you have an opportunity to influence their enjoyment of music throughout life.

Rhythm Time

Young children need the opportunity to develop the rhythms they feel and hear. Along with providing an inner satisfaction, this activity helps develop physical coordination, auditory discrimination, and self-control. There are many books and records that provide the music needed, but the best experiences are those which prompt a spontaneous and creative response. With a piano or other instrument, you can play rhythmic patterns that encourage galloping, flying, skating, marching, tiptoeing, walking, hopping, etc. Fast and slow patterns can be incorporated with any of the above.

Rhythmic activity with songs that children already know adds another dimension. "Clap" the rhythm instead of singing the words; then "step" or "hop" the rhythm.

Traditional folk games, passed from generation to generation, help to develop the ability to follow directions and provide action, so they're good choices for young children. Some well known ones are "Did You Ever See A Lassie," "Looby Loo," and "Skip To My Lou."

There are many excellent rhythm activity records available; some incorporate simple props, such as scarves. You should always be familiar with the material and have props on hand before you present it.

Traditional folk games, passed from generation to generation, help to develop the ability to follow directions and provide action, so they're good choices for young children.

Rhythm instruments offer an opportunity for creative activity. These can be used for special effects in certain songs or as an additional activity in playing rhythm patterns. The activities should be exploratory and spontaneous, not a "planned" activity, such as a teacher directing a rhythm band.

Fingerplays and Activity Poems

Fingerplays and activity poems are an enjoyable multi-level activity for your students. They extend the attention span, help develop auditory discrimination, enlarge the vocabulary, and augment a sense of rhythm. For you, they're a technique for getting and keeping control, for easing transition times, and for getting children on their feet and freeing them of their wiggles.

To teach a fingerplay or activity poem, say and do the finger and/or body movement, then ask the students to do as you do. Make sure you know the material well before presenting it.

It's useful to develop a card file of fingerplays and activity poems. These can be categorized by the time of year, subject matter, or length and complexity. Many of our favorites can be found in the Resource Section.

We have searched for sources of the fingerplays, with no success. They seem to be like folk songs—handed from one person to the next.

Snack Time

> *Snack time is a good time to introduce elementary manners—washing hands before eating, eating slowly, cleaning the table after eating.*

Like everything else, snack time serves more than one purpose:
1. It is nutritious;
2. It is a learning experience;
3. Its preparation involves the children to some degree;
4. It is unscheduled (usually a choice during worktime).

Cookies and milk are at best a thing of the past, or at least just an occasional treat. Snacks with higher protein content give a greater and more lasting energy boost than sweets. Peanut butter and crackers, little squares of cheese, and vegetables with dip are favorites.

Snack time is a good time to introduce elementary manners—washing hands before eating, eating slowly, cleaning the table after eating.

Preparation can involve mathematical experiences. Preparers can count the children present, then fill that many small cups with popcorn. They can count so many crackers per snacker.

Think of the snack as more beneficial if the children can decide when to snack—this usually works better than setting a specific time when everyone stops other activities so that the entire class can snack. At first, this will take a bit more effort on your part, but it's better to have the snacks available in a designated area and allow children to snack when they please during worktime. The spontaneous snack involves teaching expectations and learning to live up to those expectations. If only one snack is allowed, that expectation must be followed. Close observation is necessary at first, but the children adjust to the expectations in a short time. Do not sell that adjustment short. You are helping the children develop self-control and self-reliance.

Some teachers, however, prefer a scheduled snack time to stress good manners, waiting for everyone to be served, serving as host or hostess, and sharing a birthday treat. Do what works best for you and your class.

Game Time

A teaching technique compatible with our early childhood philosophy is the "game" approach. Games are an informal and spontaneous way of providing experiences that serve to promote social development, muscular growth, and self-control; some also serve as foundations for reading, writing, and mathematics.To the casual observer, the activity might appear to be "play"; to the kindergarten teacher, the game is a structured, appropriate learning activity of great value which she can justify.

Games ease the transition between active and quiet experiences. Many five-minute games help get the children on their feet for an activity change.

Some games can be explained completely in advance; others may need to be explained step-by-step when introduced. Teaching techniques can add to the value of the game. When talking with students about voice level during a game, introduce the idea of "inside" and "outside" voices as a means of volume control. The "inside" voice does not use the volume that the "outside" voice uses. "Use your 'inside' voice," is more positive than "Don't be so loud." Play most games with the children; you'll enhance the situation and help develop an attitude of enjoyment. If a game is not truly enjoyed, it is not a good game.

Foster and Headey in *Education in the Kindergarten* observe:

"Games best adapted to kindergarten play are those which are loosely organized; frequently they are of the 'ring' or 'circle' type. The games are not dependent on a specific number of players or a permanent casting of parts. There is some evidence that competition begins to be a stimulating factor in the activities of the five-year-old; but that does not mean that it should be stressed in group games. At age five there is still little if any team feeling; competition is pretty much a matter of personal concern. 'Our side' and 'your side' mean very, very little to the kindergarten child."

Simple games that include all the children are the most suitable; "Here We Go Round the Mulberry Bush," "Looby Loo," and "Musical Chairs" are good examples. Imitative games such as "Simple Simon" and "Follow the Leader" include all the children at the same time.

Games that have a series of actions in sequence, like "Farmer in the Dell," can begin with two "farmers" to increase the number of children involved.

A shy child who hesitates to participate in a game may be allowed to observe for a while. If you participate in the game, it is helpful to have that child at your side. A child can learn by watching and, when comfortable, will participate without urging.

Different games provide different types of experiences. Some stress concentration or alertness, while others stress memory, strategy, guessing, development of motor skills and/or special integration. Keep in mind the needs of the students and incorporate a variety of games that meet those needs into the curriculum.

Play most games with the children; you'll enhance the situation and help develop an attitude of enjoyment. If a game is not truly enjoyed, it is not a good game.

Building Partnerships with Other Adults

The kindergarten teacher who puts her best foot forward with colleagues, parents, and the community is an asset to her school system and makes her own job easier. You should consider yourself and your program as constantly on view and representative of your profession.

Working with Colleagues

Assume responsibility for:

1. Explaining your program;
2. Helping to take the pressure off the upper grade teachers;
3. Adding to the atmosphere of the school.

Try to impress upon everyone within earshot that continuous progress is what you and your colleagues seek.

Kindergarten is the beginning of so much that happens to children, and some of your classroom preparation can start in the teachers' lounge. Don't fall into the habit of taking your frustrations to the lounge—the lounge should be a haven, a brief respite from the less-than-desirable aspects of the day.

Help set the stage in the lounge just as you do in your classroom. Perhaps you can be the one who suggests that conversation exclude children, parents, and school. Just think of the time that leaves for subjects like clothes, diets, restaurants, movies, plays, recreation, the arts, and jokes! There's no limit to how much a few moments focused on these topics can refresh your day. For twelve years, it was our pleasure to work at a school that had a "no school talk in the lounge" policy. It was wonderful. Try it, you'll like it!

Are we being unkind to the frustrated teacher? Perhaps there's another area for sounding off. If there must be occasional griping, so be it, but it's better to sound off where it counts—at faculty meetings or privately to your superior. A gripe ceases to be a gripe when it offers an alternative. Otherwise, it is a continuation of the problem instead of a solution. Trust us, administrators appreciate any alternatives which help them help children.

Be of special help to the teacher who follows you. We believe that some first-grade teachers have to face unrealistic expectations from parents and administrators. Try to impress upon everyone within earshot that continuous progress is what you and your colleagues seek.

Working with Administrators

We have never known an administrator who did not appreciate being given an article or book that helped him grow. Do not write off a superior because he or she came from a secondary school, or coached, or for any other reasons we have heard. If your administrator does not visit your room much, it may be because he is uncomfortable there. That's understandable and avoidable if you offer some help. Invite him to your room for specific activities. Before or after the visit, explain the value of what you have done. It will not take many visits for him to understand the rationale behind what you are doing, and he'll be able to explain it to others. Give him early childhood articles and books to read and you'll soon have a strong, informed, understanding ally. The time you invest will bring returns tenfold.

Working with Parents

A strong school has parents and teachers working as partners with one goal—giving each child the best. If anything in our profession has been underestimated, it is the importance of a congenial, positive relationship with parents. Give serious thought to having the pre-school conference. Once you have enjoyed the fruits of that endeavor and your colleagues hear how it has been valuable to you, they might try it. What a great trend to start!

If anything in our profession has been underestimated, it is the importance of a congenial, positive relationship with parents.

After your initial contact with parents, concentrate on keeping them informed throughout the year. Some ways to do this include:

Bulletins

At the start of the school year, parents appreciate written information about school hours, supplies needed, how clothing should be marked, lost and found procedures, and other school policies and practices. Throughout the year, additional bits of necessary "nuts and bolts" information can be handled via bulletins.

Parents' Meeting

In most areas, this meeting takes place during "Back to School Night." Because it is difficult for parents with several children to attend all sessions, some school systems save the kindergarten meeting for another night. It is an accepted practice for the administrator to start the meeting with a welcome and a suggestion that this is a night reserved for general information, not a night to discuss individual children. In order for this to not be considered a "put off," it is important to add that parents who have particular concerns are welcome to schedule a private conference to be held at a later date.

The best way to assure a productive partnership with parents is to inform them that they are welcome to visit at anytime.

Meeting agenda:

1. Have a copy of your daily schedule and talk the parents through an entire session.
2. Explain the rationale behind each experience or activity and its social, emotional, intellectual, and creative value.
3. Explain the appropriate ways you expose children to, and teach them, reading, writing and math.
4. Explain the school's visitation and conference procedure.
5. Give suggestions about what they can do at home to help the school experience. A few examples:
   a. They can read stories to the children—a good pre-bedtime activity.
   b. They can take the children along on errands (a way to expand and give meaning to the child's vocabulary).
   c. They can talk to you or your administrator about concerns.
6. Leave time for questions. Don't be afraid to say "I don't know, but I'll find out and let you know."

Newsletters

Newsletters are good public relations and another way of assuring that parents understand your program. They can be written regularly or at any time which seems appropriate. Newsletters can include:

1. Themes which have been covered and interesting related activities.
2. Themes to be covered and planned related activities.
3. Requests for specific materials needed for crafts (toilet paper rolls, wax paper rolls, bottle caps, buttons, etc.).
4. Specific math activities which are being used.
5. Specific reading activities, including stories which have been read to the children.
6. Songs the children have learned.
7. Suggestions about helpful activities at home.
8. An invitation to visit.

Visiting the Classroom

The best way to assure a productive partnership with parents is to inform them that they are welcome to visit at anytime. In some areas, safety precautions such as signing in at the office are required. If parents can drop in without an appointment or specific arrangements, they usually become more supportive of the program.

There are practices that keep parent visits from being a burden to the teacher:

1. Inform parents in advance (perhaps at the parent meeting) that they are welcome at any time without pre-arrangement.
2. Inform them that you might nod but you will not interrupt the program to greet them or have their children perform.
3. Ask them to:
   a. Observe the program;
   b. Not interrupt the flow of the day;
   c. Not try and have a conversation with the teacher;
   d. Call for an appointment for a conference if anything needs clarification while you are interacting with the children.
4. Stress that what they will see is exactly what would be going on if there were no visitors.

This last condition, if you will adhere to it, will make the visit just something else that is happening. You have made no special plans for it. *What's good enough for the children is good enough for the world to see.*

Occasional Notes

Many treasured scrapbooks contain notes with messages such as "How John grew today! He wanted to play with the big blocks but didn't get a turn. He handled the situation well." Or, "How I wish you could have seen Mary's block work today. She was so creative." You can put these messages on small pieces of paper headed "Good News Note."

Report Cards

We believe that the primary grades are a bit early for report cards and we are seeing changes throughout the country in this area; individualized written evaluations instead of letter grades provide a better measure of the child's progress. However, in many districts report cards are mandated or expected. If you have any influence on the content of report cards (never underestimate your influence!), we hope you will encourage reasonable expectations and helpful information. "Unsatisfactory," "needs to improve," and "below level" are not suitable ways of reporting or helping the very young. If there has to be some kind of evaluation, we suggest using the following phrases instead:

Most of the time (who is perfect always?).

Sometimes (he is getting there).

Not yet (we expect the best eventually).

A conference can be personal and in-depth; we prefer conferences to report cards.

A conference can be personal and in-depth; we prefer conferences to report cards.

Conferences

Ideally, the pre-school conference has established a relationship which fosters easy communication throughout the year. It is usually adequate to have scheduled conferences in November and March but helpful to say that anytime you or parent want a conference, one can be scheduled.

There is a trend toward giving teachers release time for conferences. We feel this is only fair, given the importance of parent involvement in children's education.

Assure the parents you are willing to work with them on any areas of concern.

A good procedure:

1. If you do not have release time, try not to schedule a conference immediately after school. Give yourself a few minutes to rest and refresh yourself.
2. Try to see both parents if possible. Many businesses are very good about giving parents release time to go to school for a conference.
3. Smile as the parents enter the room. They will feel more at ease and free to talk to you.
4. Start with the good things you can say about the child. However, if you have a concern, you owe it to the parents to give them that information. So often it is not *what* is said but *how* it is said that can be offensive, so choose your words carefully.
5. Don't do all the talking. Give parents time to express concerns to each other and ask questions.
6. Assure the parents you are willing to work with them on any areas of concern.
7. Try to avoid the use of such words as "immature," "emotional problem," etc. These words can easily be misinterpreted by parents and can damage the relationship.
8. Don't allow yourself to get trapped into an argument. You might win an argument but lose a chance to help a child. If the situation gets tense, try to close the conference and schedule another one after a cooling-off period.
9. Close on a positive note. Thank the parents for coming, tell them you appreciate their interest in their child, and remind them you will help in any way you can. Leave the door open for any future conferences or visits they might desire.

Working with an Aide

In our opinion, having a paid aide is an investment that gets the highest return on a dollar. In addition to lowering the adult-pupil ratio, an aide increases the teacher's effectiveness in the classroom.

In a smooth operation, the casual observer might have a difficult time telling who is the teacher and who is the aide, because both are interacting with the children in the same manner. The big difference is in the behind-the-scenes planning; it is the teacher who makes the plans. If a teacher is fortunate enough to have the same aide for a period of time, there can be discussion and an interchange of ideas, but the buck will always stop with the teacher. The teacher can teach her aide how to read a story to the children, for example, but the teacher picks the story.

If you have an aide, you have two responsibilities—diagnosing the instructional needs of your students, and training your aide to help meet those needs. You will find your time well spent.

The climate for the children is going to be even better if there is a congenial relationship between aide and teacher. This is best accomplished by following the advice, "Don't make a maid of the aide." If teacher and aide share the less-than-desirable tasks, the aide will retain appropriate self-esteem.

The most important instruction you can give an aide is that she do nothing for the children that they can do for themselves. Guiding them might take more time, but taking responsibility is an important part of children's growth.

If teacher and aide share the less-than-desirable tasks, the aide will retain appropriate self-esteem.

Aides can:

Greet children and help them start their day smoothly
Visit with the children
Discuss their work with them
Give simple forms of first aid
Assist with wraps, etc., at the end of the day
Reinforce directions if necessary
Respond to children's requests for help
Read stories to an individual or small group
Oversee proper use and return of materials
Help make visual aids and teaching materials
Help with preparation for the day
Mix paint
Keep track of helper charts
Check the usable supplies (crayons, paper, paint, etc.)

If you have the same aide throughout the year, she can be a good substitute teacher if you must be absent (state statutes might prohibit this practice). A substitute aide can be hired in her place, and the continuity is not disturbed because your aide is familiar with all procedures and children.

Perhaps you think it should go without saying, but say it:

1. The aide does not discuss sensitive school issues when in the community.

2. When parents ask the aide about children, she is to refer them to the teacher.

Not all teachers are fortunate enough to have a paid aide, and with so many working mothers it is hard to get volunteers, ***but it's worth a try.*** One resourceful teacher recruited five mothers—one for each day of the week. She made job cards of things they could do to help. Since each mother came on the same day each week, she became accustomed to the routine and was a tremendous help. It required terrific effort from the teacher in the beginning, but it enhanced her class throughout the year.

The most important instruction you can give an aide is that she do nothing for the children that they can do for themselves.

Resources

We recommend teaching the "The Three Rules Song" on the first day of class:

At school [clap, clap, clap]
We have three rules [clap, clap, clap]
First, finish all your work each day,
Sec-ond, put your things away,
The third rule, let me hear you say,
Don't bug your buddy,
No, don't bug your buddy

Bulletin Boards

Bulletin boards emphasize and enhance the topics you're covering in the classroom. There are bulletin board idea books available that concentrate on young children; commercial materials for bulletin boards are also abundant. You might want to adapt an idea to accommodate a particular class and use some commercial material combined with your own creative ideas and the work of the children.

The following ideas are listed in a monthly sequence; they're only suggestions. Because putting up bulletin boards can be time-consuming, we offer these thoughts:

1. Develop basic background color schemes for the year;
2. Begin with fall colors: yellow, orange, green, tan, and brown. These can be used through Thanksgiving.
3. In December change to white, red, and green;
4. In February change the green to blue;
5. For the final three months, use spring and pastel colors.

Bulletin boards should reflect the unit studies and interests of the children. They should provide a background to display work or actually be the work, e.g, a mural.

SEPTEMBER

1. Theme: Fall
Background: Yellow
Preparation:
Teacher: Large tree with either leaves, apples, or acorns falling to the ground. Write each child's name on individual symbols; make name tags in the shape of the symbol used.

2. Theme: Welcome
Background: Orange or yellow
Preparation:
Teacher: Put up background with the words "Welcome" or "Our Bunch" across the board.
Students: Draw a picture of themselves on a piece of 9" x 12" manila paper, cut out, and put on board.

3. Theme: Colors
Background: Tan
Preparation:
Teacher: A clown holding colored balloons, or a boy or girl blowing colored bubbles, or a seal bouncing colored balls on its nose. Write color names on each color.

OCTOBER

1. Theme: Halloween
Background: Neutral
Preparation:
Teacher: Cut triangles for jack-o-lantern eyes and nose and mouth shape from black construction paper. Cut the word "BOO" from black paper and put on board.
Students: Make chains from orange construction paper strips 1" x 6". Form chains into a giant pumpkin; use short green chain made from strips for stem.
2. Theme: Halloween
Background: Tan
Preparation:
Students: Draw Halloween symbols on the tan background before it is put up. Use magic markers and when it's complete, cover it with a black wash.
3. Theme: Halloween
Background: Orange
Preparation:
Teacher: Black border and word "BOO" in black.
Students: Stuff paper bags lightly with newspapers. Use a tagboard strip or stick and tie the bottom of sack around the stick. Use scraps of colored paper to make scary designs on bags. Put on board.

NOVEMBER

1. Theme: Thanksgiving
Background: Brown
Preparation:
Teacher: Shape a turkey body, front view, from a brown paper bag; stuff with newspaper, make a wattle and beak. Cut the word "gobble" from orange paper.
Students: Bring an old necktie from home to form a fan tail.
2. Theme: Fall Leaves
Background: Tan or White
Preparation:
Teacher: Make large tree with branches.
Students: Make fall leaves by either dipping hand into paint and placing on tree or trace around their hands using construction paper in fall colors (fingers can be either separated or together). Cut out and put on tree.

3. Theme: Smile
Background: Yellow
Preparation:
Teacher: Attach mirror at students' eye level.
Students: Cut smiling faces from magazines and pin on board.
4. Theme: Horn of Plenty
Background: Tan or yellow
Preparation:
Teacher: Make large horn of plenty.
Students: Students make items to go in horn of plenty; vegetables, fruits, nuts, etc. Encourage the students to make them large.

DECEMBER

1. Theme: Christmas
Background: White
Preparation:
Students: Fold each corner of a 4" square of green construction paper to the center; fold back each point and form a picture frame. Cut a scene from an old Christmas card and paste in the center. Mount on bulletin board in shape of a tree.
2. Theme: Symbols of Hanukkah
Background: Blue or white
Preparation:
Students: As children study legends, they make symbols—dreidel, menorah, and Star of David—to be displayed on the bulletin board.
3. Theme: Christmas
Background: White
Preparation:
Students: Make green chains from 1" x 6" strips. Form chains in the shape of a large Christmas tree.
4. Theme: Toy Shop
Background: White
Preparation:
Teacher: Section off board with black strips of paper to suggest windows. Add red letters that spell "Toy Shop."
Students: Use paper and scissors to make and cut out large toys to be placed in the "windows."

JANUARY

1. Theme: Mitten Time
Background: White
Preparation:
Teacher: Letters that spell "Mitten Time." Bright yarn to serve as a clothes line.
Students: On a 9" x 12" piece of construction paper (students use different colors) student traces around each hand. The pair must be colored alike. Cut out and hang on the "line."

2. Theme: Snow Scene
Background: Blue
Preparation:
Teacher: Draw three circles on white paper for snowman. Have real scarf or make paper one and hat.
Students: Tear around circles and mount on board. Use scraps of paper for face. Pin white cotton balls or white styrofoam packing bits all over the board.
3. Theme: Snow Flakes
Background: 12" x 18" multi-colored construction paper, overlapping in an irregular pattern.
Preparation:
Students: Fold 8" square of white paper and cut snowflake designs to decorate the board.

FEBRUARY

1. Theme: Flag
Background: White
Preparation:
Teacher: Mark out flag with pencil, 40" x 26". Put blue field, 10" x 14" in upper left hand corner.
Students: Make red chains from 6" x 3/4" strips to use for red stripes. Make 50 white stars to pin on the blue.
2. Theme: Valentine
Background: White
Preparation:
Teacher: Large red or pink heart on board.
Students: Take small strips of red, pink and/or white crepe paper and twist into a bow; glue onto large heart on board.
3. Theme: Valentine
Background: White
Preparation:
Teacher: Make two red hearts of different sizes. Turn the larger heart upside down for a body shape and place the smaller one on top for a "head." Make eyes, nose, and ears. Arms are small hearts overlapping the middle of the large heart, forming arms that hold a white envelope with the word "mail" on it. Large letters on the board say "Valentine Greetings." Cut smaller hearts and put the children's names on them.

MARCH

1. Theme: Fly a Kite
Background: Light blue
Preparation:
Teacher: Cut easel paper into kite shapes and cut letters that say "Go Fly a Kite."
Students: Paint and/or color kites. Attach yarn for a tail, with bow shapes cut from construction paper scraps and attached to yarn. Put on board.
2. Theme: How Will March Go Out?
Background: Blue or yellow

Preparation:

Teacher: Make a lion's head using tan or orange paper. Dimension can be added by curling strips of the same color paper and using them for a mane. Place on one side of the bulletin board. Make a lamb's head from white paper and cotton, and fasten to the other side of the board. Cut out letters to read "How will March go out? Like a lion or like a lamb?"

APRIL

1. Theme: Springtime Flowers
Background: Blue or yellow
Preparation:
Teacher: Green grass along the bottom. Cut flower shapes from newsprint easel paper.
Students: Color flower shapes with crayons, magic markers, or paint. Cut stems and leaves from green construction paper. Put on board.

2. Theme: Spring Mural
Background: Blue, yellow, or white
Preparation:
Students: Color a mural of spring activities such as trees budding, planting a garden, dogwoods, tulips, and pansies in bloom, etc., using crayons or magic markers.

3. Theme: Easter
Background: Pastel color
Preparation:
Teacher: Make a large basket from brown construction paper, or paint on easel paper and cut out. Place on board with letters that say "Happy Easter." Use Easter grass in basket.
Students: Make and color paper Easter eggs and put in basket.

MAY

1. Theme: Garden Time
Background: Pastel, tan, or white
Preparation:
Teacher: Letters that say "Garden Time," "Vegetables," "Flowers," and "Fruit."
Students: Cut out pictures of fruits, vegetables, and flowers from seed catalogues and/or seed packages. Categorize and put on board under appropriate label.

2. Theme: Maypole
Background: Pastel
Preparation:
Teacher: Cover a yardstick with crepe paper, using a contrasting color to the background, and place in the center of the bulletin board. Alternate different colored streamers (at least five) on each side of the pole. Cut out letters that say "Go Round and Round the Maypole."

3. Theme: Summer Travel
Background: Pastel or white
Preparation:
Students: Have students do a mural of where they plan to go during the summer, or where they would like to go; or have them do individual pictures that include a story sentence.

Unit Themes

Unit themes, which focus on a particular concept or topic, encourage discussing and understanding. The suggested unit themes follow the schedule of the school year; the decision about what to use and when is yours.

The format we have used includes understandings to be conveyed, appropriate worktime activities, and ideas for opening theme discussions. Many of the unit themes include a culminating activity and we have left room for notes for future references.

The units at the beginning of the school year have fewer worktime interest suggestions; the activities are expanded each week.

Introduce each activity thoroughly, and have only those activities in the room which the children will be using.

Incorporate parents when possible; use them as a resource but keep involvement on the child's level and in appropriate proportion.

Resource materials should be readily available; be prepared with more than time will allow. Keeping notes will provide an additional resource for the future.

LEARNING ABOUT OUR SCHOOL

UNDERSTANDINGS

School is our special place where we will learn many things.

We have three rules.

We have secret signals.

There are times when we choose what we do during work time.

WORKTIME INTEREST

Crayons

Beads

Pegs

UNIT DISCUSSION

The name of our school.

The names of our friends.

Secret signals.

Use of and selection process of work time interest.

Use of the bathroom

Where and when.

Turn signal at door.

Wash hands.

Change signal.

NOTES:

LEARNING ABOUT OUR KINDERGARTEN

UNDERSTANDINGS

Most things are always in the same place.

We practice how to sit, listen, and follow the rules.

We have centers—some change, some stay the same.

WORKTIME INTEREST

Crayons

Beads

Pegs

Pretend corner

Small blocks

Cut and paste shapes

UNIT DISCUSSION

How we return materials at clean-up time.

How we listen at game time.

How we can learn each other's names.

Listen during taking of attendance.

Ask the names of friends sitting by you.

NOTES:

SCHOOL HELPERS

UNDERSTANDINGS

Helpers make our school work well.

Each helper in the school has a special job.

We have helpers in our room.

WORKTIME INTEREST

Draw and color pictures of helpers, the school

Beads

Pegs

Clay

Puzzles

Cut and paste picker stickers

UNIT DISCUSSION

Discuss helpers: principal, secretary, custodian.

Visit the office to meet principal and clerk.

Introduce job chart and "office helper" idea, and let one or two children take attendance to office.

NOTES:

SAFETY

UNDERSTANDINGS

School can be a safe place.

Why we don't run, hit, or throw things.

We must follow all safety rules.

School guards are our friends; we must do as they say.

WORKTIME INTEREST

Easel painting

Blocks

Crayons

Beads

Pegs

Clay

Pretend corner

Make stop light using shoe box

School bus

UNIT DISCUSSION

Let students "make up":

Rules to follow when walking to school.

Rules to follow when riding to school by bus or car.

Discuss:

How the school guards help us.

How we help the school guard.

CULMINATING ACTIVITY

Invite school guard to talk to class.

NOTES:

ALL ABOUT ME

UNDERSTANDINGS

Each child is unique.

Being different is okay.

We are all more alike than different.

WORKTIME INTEREST

Height chart.

Full mirror for drawing self-portrait.

Trace around child and color.

UNIT DISCUSSION

Similarities and differences:

How are we alike, e.g. hair, eyes, etc.?

How are we different?
Individual self-description while looking in mirror.
NOTES:

NUTRITION

UNDERSTANDINGS
Some foods help us grow, some do not.
The four food groups that are good for us.
Foods that do not help us grow are called junk foods.
WORKTIME INTEREST
Classification of food groups.
Tasting session: opposites, sweet and sour.
Setting up grocery store.
UNIT DISCUSSION
What is your favorite food?
What foods can you fix for yourself?
What would you choose for a snack; identify food group?
CULMINATING ACTIVITY
Visit a grocery store.
NOTES:

COOKING UNIT

UNDERSTANDINGS
Some foods we eat the way they are, some we cook, some both.
Mixing food items together changes the look and taste.
Heat changes food.
WORKTIME INTEREST
Cooking from picture recipes.
Taste some food raw and cooked.
Measuring cups and spoons in sand, water table or big pan.
Child dictates a recipe for cook book.
Color, paint, or draw someone eating a favorite food.
UNIT DISCUSSION
Why we cook.

Safety rules when cooking.
What is a recipe?
CULMINATING ACTIVITY
Visit a bakery.
NOTES:

THE FAIR

UNDERSTANDINGS
The fair is an important event in the community.
People work all year to get ready for the fair.
There are many animals at the fair including baby animals.
The fair has many colors, sights, and sounds.
WORKTIME INTEREST
Make ribbons used in judging.
Cut barn shapes; students add animals, color or paste.
Mural of the fair.
Add animals to block area.
Bake cookies and judge.
UNIT DISCUSSION
What you see at the fair.
Why people bring their animals, food and crafts to the fair.
Color of ribbons at the fair.
Care of animals while they are at the fair.
CULMINATING ACTIVITY
Take a trip to the fair.
NOTES:

HALLOWEEN

UNDERSTANDINGS
Halloween is a special holiday.
Halloween can be a time for fun.
Halloween has certain rules for manners and safety.
WORKTIME INTEREST
Orange and black paint at easels.
Color pictures and cover with black wash.
Make hobgoblins.
Make black spiders using construction paper.
Make ghosts from tissues or sheets.

Make masks.

Trick or treat sack.

UNIT DISCUSSION

Read story about Halloween.

Discuss what students are going to do on Halloween night.

Safety is important at this time; discuss adults checking treats and strangers.

We do not run.

Manners to observe: walk on sidewalk, say "thank you" for a treat, etc.

CULMINATING ACTIVITY

Halloween party at school.

Visit a costume shop.

NOTES:

FALL

UNDERSTANDINGS

Fall is one of the four seasons; it follows summer.

Fall is the season that warns us that cold weather is coming.

Many changes are taking place out of doors.

WORKTIME INTEREST

Nature walk; choose a tree to observe all year.

Press leaves between wax paper.

Hand tree: have child trace around hand on construction paper; cut and mount on large brown tree on bulletin board.

Preserve leaves by dipping in warm water to which three or four teaspoons of glycerine have been added.

Crayon rubbings.

Use crayon shavings to press between wax paper; cut in leaf shapes.

Leaf spatter painting.

UNIT DISCUSSION

Read about fall.

What time of year is fall?

How you can tell when fall is here?

Why leaves loose their green color?

Name all the colors in fall leaves.

Another word that tells us what season it is?

CULMINATING ACTIVITY

Visit a park.

Visit a nature center.

NOTES:

INDIANS

UNDERSTANDINGS

Indians were the very first Americans.
The Indians lived in this country before Pilgrims came.
Pilgrims were people who came to America from England.
The Indians helped the Pilgrims.

WORKTIME INTERESTS

Indian "tom-toms" from round boxes (oatmeal or salt).
Indian headbands using brown paper, crayons, and construction paper for feathers.
Tepees from round circles of construction paper.
Class mural.

UNIT DISCUSSION

Who were the first people in America?
How did Indians help Pilgrims?
How did the Indians live?
What did they eat?
What did they wear?
How did they send messages?
Are Indians still in America today?

CULMINATING ACTIVITY

Visit museum with exhibition on Indian culture.
Invite a person of Indian heritage to talk with class.

NOTES:

THANKSGIVING

UNDERSTANDINGS

Thanksgiving is an American holiday which the Pilgrims started.
They invited friendly Indians to the celebration.
Americans still celebrate Thanksgiving about the time farmers harvest their crops.
Why we use the traditional foods for Thanksgiving dinner.

WORKTIME INTERESTS

Pilgrim hats.
Mural of large table with food.
On paper plates or large circles, color or cut and paste foods we select for our dinner.
Trace around hand for turkey shape (thumb is head, fingers are the tail feathers).

Pop corn.
Cooking center prepares food for "feast" last day before holiday.

UNIT DISCUSSION

Read Thanksgiving story.
Why did Pilgrims have a celebration?
Who came?
How do we celebrate today?
Do we eat at home?
Do we invite people?
What do we eat; is it like the first Thanksgiving?
Can we have a Thanksgiving feast at school?
Why are we thankful?

CULMINATING ACTIVITY

Thanksgiving feast.
Each student states why he is thankful.

NOTES:

WINTER

UNDERSTANDINGS

Winter follows fall season.
When it's cold we wear more clothes.
Animals and birds grow their coats.
Some animals hibernate, some store food, some go south.
Changes in the home—heat.

WORKTIME INTEREST

Paintings and colorings of squirrels and bears.
Family dressed for winter.
Make bird feeder.
Collect old sheets to make head scarves. Color on designs and press with warm iron.
Trace around hands for mittens; cut out and decorate.

UNIT DISCUSSION

Tell me anything you know about winter.
How does your family get ready for winter?
How do animals get ready for winter?

NOTES:

CHRISTMAS AND HANUKKAH

UNDERSTANDINGS

People celebrate holidays according to what they believe.
Christmas and Hanukkah are fun times but also serious.
Most families do things together during the holiday.
We can make presents for those we love.

WORKTIME INTEREST

Prepare holiday gift.
Decorations such as painted bells from paper cups.
Red and green chains for Christmas, and blue and white chains for Hanukkah.
Make greeting cards for those we love.
Cut easel paper in shape of tree.
Star of David from triangles.
Make wrapping paper (block prints from sponge or potato).
Menorah using pattern.

UNIT DISCUSSION

Utilize parents or community members to explain celebrations.
How does your family celebrate?
What do you do to get ready for the holidays?
What do we do for others at this time, e.g. food drives,
filling stockings for needy, etc.?
What is a secret; do you know how to keep a secret?
We want to keep the gift we make a secret.

CULMINATING ACTIVITY

Visit a toy store.

NOTES:

A NEW YEAR AND TIME

UNDERSTANDINGS

January first begins a new calendar year.
Our year has a new number.
There are long and short periods of time—months, days, hours, etc.
Clocks tell us when to get up, come to school, go home, etc.
January is "winter" time.

WORKTIME INTEREST

Make January calendar.
Clock faces of paper plates.
Make four "seasons" booklet.

UNIT DISCUSSION

What is the new number for the new year.
What is the name of new month.
Count weeks in new month.
Count and name days of week.
How many hours in a day (use clock to demonstrate).
How many hours at school.
What time do you get up, go to bed.

NOTES:

TOYS

UNDERSTANDINGS

It is fun to share our experiences from the holidays with our friends at school. New toys are part of these experiences.
Some toys need more than one person.
Taking care of toys will make them last.
Toys don't always have to be purchased.

WORKTIME INTEREST

Introduce woodworking. Put a few wheels at the bench so children can make toys.
Creative picture—Me with my favorite toy.
Make "Toy Book"—each child makes picture of favorite toy to be put together in a book.
Red wagon; cut and paste with black wheels.

CULMINATING ACTIVITY

Toy day; each child brings their favorite toy *to share.*

NOTES:

SNOW

Use only if there is snow

UNDERSTANDINGS

What is going on outside.
Snow falls during cold weather.
Snow is different from rain and sleet.
Chemical change.
Why we dress differently.

WORKTIME INTEREST

Cut snow flakes.
Easel paper in shape of snowman.
Creative pictures.
Whipped soap snow.

Snowman, white paint on blue paper.
Winter scenes, dark blue paper with white (chalk, paint, sponge, or easel).
Snow mural.
Make snow ice cream; add food coloring.
Put snow in water table, observe change.

UNIT DISCUSSION

Is it easy to move about in the snow?
How does the city help when there is snow?
Does the city have rules about the snow?
Is it still safe to drive?
How can we have fun in the snow?
What is a snow shovel, how is it different?
What happens when we bring snow inside?
Where do you put your snow clothes when you come inside?

NOTES:

WHERE WE LIVE

UNDERSTANDINGS

Houses are not all alike.
Different people live different ways.
Why we have an address.

WORKTIME INTEREST

Put wooden people in block area.
Shoe box houses.
Mural of a street with houses of children.
Individual pictures of child's house with address.
Fold paint paper in fourths and color each a room at home.

UNIT DISCUSSION

Discuss different kinds of houses.
Different materials used to build.
Who are the helpers needed to build a house?
Tell about houses on your block.
Why do we have addresses?

NOTES:

HEALTH AND SAFETY AT HOME

UNDERSTANDINGS

Staying clean helps us stay well.
When we are sick, we rest and do what our parents say.
When growing, we need sleep.
There are safety rules at home.

WORKTIME INTEREST

Opposite pictures (what is good for us, what is not).
Creative painting and coloring of safety pictures.
Teach poem about sneezing; have copy for child to take home.

> "Whenever you have to sneeze,
> Always cover your mouth, please."

Illustrate what poem tells us.

UNIT DISCUSSION

What do we mean by good health?
Can anything go into our mouth?
Name foods that help us stay well.
Who takes care of us when we are sick?
What do you do when you sneeze?
Make up rules to follow when sick.
Make up safety rules for home.

NOTES:

DOCTOR AND NURSE

UNDERSTANDINGS

The doctor and nurse help us stay well; they help us to get well when we are sick.
The doctor goes to school for many years.
There are different kinds of doctors (specialization).
The nurse has special training.

WORKTIME INTEREST

Pretend corner: use white jacket, stethoscope, and flashlight.
Make reflector headbands.
Start "Helpers Book." Make using construction paper for cover and have several blank pages for coloring illustrations of the different community "helpers" e.g., doctor, dentist, fireman, etc.
Make nurse's hat.

UNIT DISCUSSION

How many have been to a doctor?

What did the doctor do?

What does a nurse do?

Where does a doctor work (office, hospital, and house calls)?

Have you ever been to a hospital?

Many years of schooling for a doctor; nurse has special training.

What is a prescription?

CULMINATING ACTIVITY

Visit a doctor or hospital.

NOTES:

DENTIST

UNDERSTANDINGS

The dentist is a doctor for our teeth. He goes to school to learn.

He teaches people how to care for their teeth.

Some foods are good for our teeth, others are not.

WORKTIME INTEREST

Reflector headbands.

In block area or pretend corner, create dentist office.

Make book of foods that are good and not good for teeth.

Start lost tooth club: large tooth shape displayed in room
that children sign when they loose a tooth.

UNIT DISCUSSION

What does a dentist do?

Does he have special machines and tools?

Has anyone had a cavity? What is a filling?

What do we do to take care of our teeth?

What are false teeth? Why do some people have them?

Discuss what foods are good/not good for teeth.

CULMINATING ACTIVITY

Visit a dentist.

NOTES:

THE FIREMAN

UNDERSTANDINGS

We really need firemen when houses catch on fire.
How to call firemen.
Firemen teach safety rules.
Firemen are brave.
People have to learn to be firemen.

WORKTIME INTEREST

If possible begin study with trip to fire station, or have a fireman visit the class.
Continue "Helpers Book."
Make fireman's hat.
Pretend fire truck with chairs or boxes.
Pretend corner becomes a fire station.

UNIT DISCUSSION

How are a fireman's clothes different?
A fireman has two homes.
He has a certain job when he is living at the fire station.
What does the truck look like?
Where does the water come from?

NOTES:

POLICEMAN

UNDERSTANDINGS

We need helpers in our room, we need helpers in our community.
The policeman is our friend and helper.
It's his job to see that people follow rules.

WORKTIME INTEREST

Large cardboard boxes—pretend cars.
Continue "Helpers Book."
Make fingerprints; have magnifying glass to observe difference.
Street with houses and your address.
Pretend corner becomes a police station.
Make hat and badge.

UNIT DISCUSSION

How are we alike (two arms, eyes, etc.,); how are we different (fingerprints)?
If you are lost and see a policeman, what would you do?

Know your address and telephone number.
How does a dog help a policeman?

CULMINATING ACTIVITY

Have policeman visit, or visit a police station.

NOTES:

POSTMAN

UNDERSTANDINGS

How letters get from place to place.
Different kinds of mail.
Why we have to use stamps.

WORKTIME INTEREST

Pretend corner becomes a post office.
Make postman hats and bags.
Group letter dictation to be mailed to principal; mark day mailed to see how long it takes before being delivered.
Bring stamps for a collection.
Draw a picture, enclose in envelope from home.
Mail to themselves.

UNIT DISCUSSION

What kind of mail do you like to get?
What does the postman do for us?
Why do people write letters?
What is a postcard?

CULMINATING ACTIVITY

Visit a post office.

NOTES:

VALENTINE'S DAY

UNDERSTANDINGS

Valentine's Day comes on February 14.
On this day we can make others happy.

WORKTIME INTEREST

Cut easel paper in heart shapes; use pink, red, and white paint.
Make valentine people.

Cut and paste valentines using old valentines, doilies, flower catalogues, wallpaper, etc.
Make valentines to take home.
Decorate valentine sacks.
Make valentine cookies.

UNIT DISCUSSION

What do you like about Valentine's Day?
How do you feel when you receive a valentine?
How can we make valentines?

CULMINATING ACTIVITY

Valentine Party; no names on envelopes, each child brings valentine for entire class.

NOTES:

GEORGE WASHINGTON

UNDERSTANDINGS

George Washington was the first president of the United States; he is known as "The Father of Our Country."
He is known for his honesty.
He was a general during the Revolutionary War.
The capital is named for him.
He had the first flag made.

WORKTIME INTEREST

Show units of money with his picture.
Rubbings using quarters.
George Washington hats.
Flags—thirteen stars.
Paper chain flag.

UNIT DISCUSSION

Discuss events in George Washington's life.
Pictures of Mount Vernon—a museum today.
Discuss Washington Memorial.
Who is president today and where does he live?
How we honor the flag; discuss symbols of colors, stripes and stars?
Homework: how many stripes and stars?

NOTES:

ABRAHAM LINCOLN

UNDERSTANDINGS

Lincoln was one of our great presidents.
He wanted very much to be educated.
How he learned to be a lawyer.
People thought he was honest.

WORKTIME INTEREST

Continue paper chain flag.
Rubbings of Lincoln penny.
Look at picture of $5 bill.
Lincoln logs.
Log cabin made from corrugated paper.
Flag with correct number of stars.

UNIT DISCUSSION

Read about Lincoln. Discuss his courage, honesty, and desire to learn.
Discuss Lincoln Memorial.

NOTES:

OUR COUNTRY

UNDERSTANDINGS

President lives in Washington, D.C.; he works with people from all states to form rules to live by.
Another word for rules is laws.
Our country is made up of people who came from other nations.
Our country is great because many people work together.

WORKTIME INTEREST

Creative pictures: flag, White House, log cabin.
Make soldier hats for parade.
Make flags for parade.
Make log cabins: pretzels, popsicle sticks, or chalk.
Uncle Sam hat.

UNIT DISCUSSION

What is the name of our country?
Define ancestor.
What was the country of your ancestors?
Who is the president today and where does he live?
Who is Uncle Sam?
How many stripes does the flag have; what do colors and stars stand for?

NOTES:

OUR STATE

Adapt what is appropriate for your state; this unit is good to use during the anniversary week of statehood.

UNDERSTANDINGS

How the state was named.

How the state was settled.

How old is the state; what number was it when it became a state.

Does the state have its own flag?

WORKTIME INTEREST

Utilize interests relevant to your state, e.g. Oklahoma had an Indian population, a land run, etc.

UNIT DISCUSSION

Find out: (homework)

State bird;

State flower;

State tree;

Song—teach if possible.

Have pictures of items unique to state to stimulate discussion.

NOTES:

EASTER AND SPRING

UNDERSTANDINGS

During spring, the world looks like it is waking up.

Flowers bloom, trees grow leaves, animals that hibernate wake up; it is a pretty time.

Spring is a time that makes people feel good.

Easter is a part of spring.

WORKTIME INTEREST

Make Easter baskets growing rye grass (see craft section).

Cook eggs and color them.

Make bunny ears.

Stained glass windows.

Make apple trees using popcorn for blossoms, red bud trees using pink tissue for buds.

Walk around outside to observe what is happening.

UNIT DISCUSSION

What "signs of spring" have you seen?

At what time of year does Easter come?

Baby animals are born in the spring.

What animals are hatched from eggs?

CULMINATING ACTIVITY

Easter egg hunt on school grounds or in a park.

NOTES:

WINDY WEATHER

UNDERSTANDINGS

Sometimes March is called the windy month.

Windy weather can bring bad weather.

There are certain rules to follow in bad weather.

Windy weather is when we fly kites.

WORKTIME INTEREST

Make construction paper kites.

Make pin wheels.

Straw paint.

Sail boats.

Fly a kite outside.

UNIT DISCUSSION

Do you like to be in the wind?

How does it affect us (blows hair, feel it, dries our skin)?

What happens to water in the wind (evaporation)?

What makes a sailboat move, a kite fly?

What is a weather vane?

What are some good things that wind does? bad things?

NOTES:

SPACE

Time with a space launch, if possible.

UNDERSTANDINGS

The place where we live is called a planet.

The name of our planet is earth.

There is a lot of space around our planet earth.

Our planet is part of a collection of planets called the solar system.

We send astronauts into outer space to explore.

There is much to learn about outer space.

The pull of gravity keeps us on the earth.

WORKTIME INTEREST

Space rocket in block area: ear phones, walkie talkies; learn countdown.

Cut and paste space rockets.

Make instant pudding in baggie; eat with straw.

Magnets on science table.

Rockets from cardboard tubes.

Create pictures of world without gravity.

UNIT DISCUSSION

What is space? Can you see it or touch it?

What is gravity? Demonstrate.

What is an astronaut?

How does he land after being in space (on land and water)?

What does he wear?

What is an orbit?

NOTES:

BIRDS

UNDERSTANDINGS

There are many different kinds of birds.

Some birds are pets.

We can help birds by providing food, water, and protection.

Birds help us by eating insects.

The national bird is the eagle.

Some birds are endangered species (explain to children).

WORKTIME INTEREST

Bird's nests and eggs from clay.

Bird's nest from string, cut straws, dried grass.

Put up humming bird feeder outside, make a bird bath.

Make bird mobiles to hang in room.

Wood at workbench to build bird houses.

UNIT DISCUSSION

What makes a bird able to fly?

How are birds born? (Have samples or pictures of different types of nests.)

What is smallest and largest bird?

Do mother and father birds care for the babies?

Can all birds fly?

What bird is the symbol of our country?

What is our state bird?

NOTES:

PETS

UNDERSTANDINGS

Pets are animals that we keep because we like them.

Some animals make good pets, some do not.

We need to know how to care for our pets.

Pets need food, water, and shelter; some require special care.

A veterinarian is a doctor for pets.

WORKTIME INTEREST

Make pet graph. (Record how many children have dogs, cats, birds, etc.)

Make turtles from paper plates.

Model pets with play dough or clay.

Create a picture (my pet and me).

Cut and paste a pet and his home, e.g., fish and fishbowl, dog and doghouse, bird and bird cage.

UNIT DISCUSSION

What is a pet?

Tell us about your pet?

Are pets big or little?

What do you do for a pet?

What happens when your pet is sick?

Does your pet ever get shots? Why?

CULMINATING ACTIVITY

Have a veterinarian visit you, or visit his office.

NOTES:

SPIDERS AND INSECTS

UNDERSTANDINGS

Spiders and insects come in different sizes and colors.

Some are good, some are harmful.

Insects have six legs, spiders have eight.

Insects and spiders come from eggs.

We need rules about spiders and insects.

WORKTIME INTEREST

Pictures of ladybugs; match dot pattern on each side.

Spiders with paper (accordion folded) legs.

Spiders with play dough as body (paint) and pipe cleaners as legs.

Thumb print insects, draw on legs, eyes, and antenna.

Blot painting using butterfly-cut paper.

Mount insects in a box for a collection, cover with plastic wrap.

Cut easel paper in shape of butterfly.

UNIT DISCUSSION

Talk about ways insects and spiders are alike and different.

Why do bees sting?

What do insects and spiders need in order to live?

What do some insects do in winter?

How do insects and spiders help us, harm us?

Identify black widow and fiddle-back spider.

CULMINATING ACTIVITY

Take a nature walk.

Visit upper level science room and observe collections.

NOTES:

PLANTS

UNDERSTANDINGS

A plant has three parts: roots, stem, and leaves.

Plants grow in many places (garden, yard, house).

Plants need air, light, and water.

Plants start in different ways: seeds, bulbs, cuttings.

WORKTIME INTEREST

Plant tomato seeds.

Make book of plants grown from seeds, bulbs, and cuttings.

Start sweet potato in water and carrot top on wet paper towel.

Plant experiment: three identical plants, withhold water from one, air from one, and light from one.

Experiment: place celery stalk or white carnation in colored water and observe during the week (aspiration).

UNIT DISCUSSION

Discuss ways plants start, three parts to plants.

Daily observation and discussion of experiments.

What types of plants do we know?

CULMINATING ACTIVITY

Visit a nursery.

NOTES:

GARDENING

UNDERSTANDINGS

Gardens give us flowers and food.

We depend on gardens for food.

Sizes of gardens (incorporate produce farms).

Gardens need care.

WORKTIME INTEREST

Mural of vegetable and/or flower garden.

Start plant by cuttings (philodendron).

Plant flowers in paper cup; zinnia, marigold, and pumpkin will germinate quickly.

Construct a scarecrow with children bringing item needed (old hat, shirt, overalls, etc.), stuff with hay.

Fold paper in thirds, cut and paste pictures that start in the different ways discussed in this unit.

UNIT DISCUSSION

What do seeds need in order to grow?

How do we care for plants?

How do we choose the place for a garden?

What do you do to get ready to plant a garden?

What happens to a garden in winter?

What would you plant in a garden?

Can you mix flowers and food plants in the same garden?

CULMINATING ACTIVITY

Start a garden at school.

Visit a nursery.

NOTES:

THE FARM

UNDERSTANDINGS

There are different kinds of farms: dairy, poultry, hog, cattle, sheep, garden and field crop, orchard, etc.

Most of the food we eat comes from a farm.

Different farms need different buildings and equipment.

Running a farm is a lot of work.

Some farm animals are useful and necessary.

Good crops depend on certain weather.

WORKTIME INTEREST

Mural of a farm.

Farm animals in block and sand table areas.

Model clay farm animals.

Booklet in shape of barn; students color animals.

Make butter: two cups whipping cream in quart jar; children take turns shaking until butter forms.

UNIT DISCUSSION

Why are farms necessary to us?

Who lives on a farm?

Helpers at harvest time.

What kinds of animals does a farmer have?

Are the baby names of animals different?

What comes from an orchard farm?

Where do wool clothes come from?

Does the produce farmer take his crop to the grocery store?

CULMINATING ACTIVITY

Visit a farm.

NOTES:

OUR ENVIRONMENT

UNDERSTANDINGS

Healthy people need good air, water, and food.

When air and water are polluted, they can make us sick.

There are things each of us can do to help keep our air and water clean.

WORKTIME INTEREST

Plant a tree.

Walk and gather litter.

Take responsibility for part of school yard.

Make litter bag for car.

UNIT DISCUSSION

What we need to keep our water clean.

What we need to keep our air clean.

When people throw things out, what does our world look like?

What is recycling?

What are some of the things people throw out of cars?

NOTES:

SHOPPING CENTER

UNDERSTANDINGS

There are many different stores in a shopping center.

It takes many helpers to run a department store.

People earn money when they work in a store.

If we want something in a store, we have to pay for it.

There is a certain way we behave when we go to a shopping center.

WORKTIME INTEREST

Construct store (big block or pretend area) with cash register, play money, and items to sell.

Mural of shopping mall.

Classification game—specific items to specific stores.
Shoe box shopping center.

UNIT DISCUSSION

How many have been to a mall?
How is it different than a store?
Name some stores in a mall.
Can you have anything when you go shopping?
How do parents pay for what they buy (cash, check, credit card)?
Discuss good manners when shopping (do not run, always ask for things, do not touch things, stay with the person you are with).

CULMINATING ACTIVITY

Visit a shopping mall.

NOTES:

THE CIRCUS

UNDERSTANDINGS

A big circus usually comes to town once a year.
It can be in a big building or a big tent.
There are many different things to see and hear.
Circus people do things you do not see done any place else.
Some things are dangerous and require a lot of practice.

WORKTIME INTEREST

Pretend corner: clown makeup.
Clown pictures using construction paper balloons with string.
Animals in circus wagon: color pictures, paste bars over them and add wheels to make circus wagon.
Have mats on floor for tricks.
Make clown hats.

UNIT DISCUSSION

How does a circus move from town to town?
Who has been to a circus?
What are some of the acts?
What animals travel with the circus and what do they do?
Who takes care of the circus animals?
Do people do more than one thing in the circus?
Who is the ringmaster?
What would you do if you could be in a circus?
Do clowns have to go to school?

CULMINATING ACTIVITY

Designate a day when everyone dresses as a circus performer.

NOTES:

THE ZOO

UNDERSTANDINGS

A zoo has animals we usually don't see anywhere else.

It takes many people to help at the zoo.

Zoo animals need special food and care.

Not all zoos have the animals in a cage; some zoos you drive through or ride in a train, and you do not get out of the car or train.

WORKTIME INTEREST

Draw animals on meat tray and make bars with yarn.

Sew around animal shapes on meat tray.

Stick puppets using popsicle sticks.

Make clay zoo animals.

Put zoo animals in block area and sand table.

Bring stuffed animal from home and create a zoo using blocks to make cages.

Splatter paint zoo animal shapes.

Collage of zoo animals.

UNIT DISCUSSION

What animals are found in a zoo?

Who takes care of the animals?

Are all animals kept in cages?

Are all cages alike?

What is a petting zoo?

Which animals are found both in the zoo and the circus?

CULMINATING ACTIVITY

Visit a zoo.

Ask a zoo worker to visit the class.

NOTES:

TRANSPORTATION

UNDERSTANDINGS

We go many places in many ways: walking, cars, buses, trains, planes, and boats. (Concentrate on forms of transportation in own area.)

Sometimes we go fast, sometimes slow.

Sometimes we travel for fun, sometimes for necessity.

You have to learn to operate different modes of transportation.

WORKTIME INTEREST

Have wood at work bench to make airplanes and wheels for trains, buses, and cars.

Make airplane from clothespin and popsicle sticks.

Add boats, ships, and canoes to water table; trucks, buses, etc. in block and sand area.

Classification: paper folded in thirds and labeled air, water, and ground. Cut and paste or draw items for each area.

Pretend corner: airplane and airport tower.

UNIT DISCUSSION

What kinds of transportation are in our town?

What makes the different kinds run?

How did people get places before cars?

Who drives in your family?

What are some parts of a car?

What are some of the things done to take care of a car?

What are rules for a passenger? Why?

What rules do you have when flying?

Why do we need beacon lights and radios at an airport?

What are boats and ships used for?

What do we call people who are in command of a boat or ship?

What are the different kinds of trains (freight, passenger, diesel, steam)?

Why do some people travel by bus?

What are some things the bus driver does?

CULMINATING ACTIVITY

Take a bus ride.

Visit an airport.

Have a senior citizen tell about the time when there were no cars.

NOTES:

EATING OUT

UNDERSTANDINGS

There are many different kinds of restaurants.

We dress differently for some types of restaurants.

We pay for food when we eat out.

We behave in a certain way.

WORKTIME INTEREST

Pretend corner or block area becomes McDonald's (McDonald's will furnish items).

Make menus for different types of restaurants.

Create a picture of your family eating out.

Classification of money (use real coins or play money).

UNIT DISCUSSION

What are some different kinds of restaurants?

How do you behave when eating out?

Do you dress differently?

Who decides what you are going to eat?

What is a children's plate?

What are some ways of behaving when we eat out; how are these different than when we eat at home?

CULMINATING ACTIVITY

Eat out as a group (possibly McDonald's).

NOTES:

VACATION TIME

UNDERSTANDINGS

We enjoy vacations when school is out.

Some vacations are at home and some are far away.

Families can plan together for summer fun.

There are health and safety rules to follow.

Pictures remind us of good times we have had.

WORKTIME INTEREST

Look at map and mark where students have been or where they are going.

Have brochures from travel agent.

Draw or cut and paste a suitcase with items to take on a trip.

Survey favorite vacation places.

Bring and share vacation pictures.

Share picture of your favorite vacation.

UNIT DISCUSSION

Why do most people go on vacation in the summer?

Can vacations come at different times during the year?

What kinds of activities do we think of in summer (swimming, picnics, boating, etc.)?

Where can we go on a vacation (in state, country, or out of the country)?

What are some good rules for summer: avoid over-exposure to sun, get enough rest, eat right, always let parents know where you are, be careful around water, etc.

CULMINATING ACTIVITY

A visit to a park.

A picnic in the park or on school grounds.

NOTES:

GETTING TO KNOW FIRST GRADE

UNDERSTANDINGS

We will learn more than we know now.

We will be in a different room.

We will stay all day; we will have lunch in the cafeteria.

WORKTIME INTEREST

Visit first grade room.
Visit first grade playground and use equipment.
Visit cafeteria and draw pictures of it.
Pretend corner: first grade room (pattern after one in your building), with paper, pencils, chalkboard, etc.

UNIT DISCUSSION

Where is the first grade room(s) in our school?
What are teachers' names?
Are any brothers or sisters in the first grade?
How do you think it will be different from kindergarten (be aware of differences according to your school)?
What is the room where we eat lunch? Do you bring or buy your lunch?
There are special helpers in the cafeteria.
Will we use the same bathrooms and fountains?

CULMINATING ACTIVITY

Spend a little time in the first grade room (possibly for a story).
Eat in the cafeteria.

NOTES:

Fingerplays and Activity Poems

Fingerplays and activity poems are used throughout the year, and even the simple ones learned in the fall are enjoyed by the children all year long. They can be used at any time during the day.

These activities provide an opportunity for a child to choose a favorite fingerplay and/or activity poem and to lead the other children in performing it. The leader experiences success, which builds self-confidence.

One way to build a convenient file is to write the poem or fingerplay down or copy the page from the book, paste individual fingerplays or activity poems on file cards, and put them in an "active" file as the children learn them.

Fingerplays

Open Them, Shut Them

Open, shut them. Open, shut them.
Give a little clap, clap, clap.
Open, shut them. Open, shut them.
Lay them in your lap, lap, lap.

Creep them, creep them, creep them,
Way up to your chin.
Open up your little mouth,
But do not let them in.

Open, shut them. Open, shut them.
To your shoulders fly,
And like little birdies,
Let them flutter to the sky.

Falling, falling, falling,
Almost to the ground,
Pick them quickly up again,
And make them go around.

Faster, faster, faster,
Slower, slower, slower,
Clap, clap, clap,
And put them in your lap.

Before Story Time

Shut your eyes,
One, two, three!
Open them and look at me.
I shall read this storybook.
Can you listen while you look?

Somebody's Birthday

Today is __________'s birthday,
Let's make her a cake. (Put hands together, palms up)
On it six (or five) candles we'll place.
Then each make a secret wish,
Blow all of them out s-s-s-swish.

Quiet Time

I know it's best
To take a rest
So I've a little key.
I'll lock the door, (children lock lips)
Pull down the shades, (Children close eyes)
I cannot talk or see!

Grandmother

Here are grandmother's glasses, (make circles around eyes)
Here is grandmother's hat. (big circle over head)
Here is the way she folds her hands,
And puts them in her lap.

The Snail

The snail lives in a curly shell, (fist)
He carries on his back,
And as he moves along the sand, (two fingers walk)
He leaves a little track.

Mr. Bullfrog

Here's Mr. Bullfrog sitting on a rock. (close left hand, with thumb up)
Along comes a little boy, (walk index and third fingers of right hand)
Mr. Bullfrog jumps, Ker flop! (dive thumb, as if into a pool)

How a Chicken Drinks

I saw a little chicken drink,
He took the water in his bill,
Then he held his head way up,
And the water ran down hill.

Houses

Here's a nest for Robin Redbreast, (cup hands)
Here is a hive for the Busy Bee. (lock all fingers together)
Here is a hole for Peter Rabbit, (touch forefinger and thumb)
And here is a house for me. (touch raised forefingers, other fingers folded)

Three Balls

Here's a ball, (thumb and forefinger of right hand touch)
A bigger ball, (touch both thumbs and middle fingers to each other)
A great big ball I see! (make circle with arms, fingers touching)
Can you count them?
Are you ready?
One, two, three. (repeat motions)

Balloons

This is the way we make a balloon,
So, so, so. (palms together)
This is the way we blow our balloon,
Blow, blow, blow. (blow into hands)
This is the way we fly our balloons,
Go, go, go. (wave hands)
This is the way we break our balloon,
Oh, oh, oh. (clap hands)

Cows

This little cow eats grass,
(index finger touches new finger on the other hand at end of each line)
This little cow eats hay,
This little cow drinks water,
But this little cow does nothing
But lie down all day.

Mother Duck and Father Drake

Two pretty ducks went swimming on the lake, (hide hands behind back)
Old Mother Duck (bring fist forward to make duck's head)
And old Father Drake (same with other hand)
"Quack," said the ducks, (open and close "bills")
"Isn't this a lovely day?"
So they dove in the water (dip hands down)
And they both swam away. (hide hands behind back.)

The Bear's Surprise

A hungry little baby bear
Went climbing up a tree.
He thought he smelled some honey there,
When out came a bee.
The bee went buzzing round and round,
And stung him on the nose.
"Oh! Dear!" said frightened Baby Bear,
"You're angry, I suppose."

This is the Bunny

This is the bunny (one hand forming a fist)
That hops so funny,
And this is his hole in the ground. (other hand, thumb and forefinger make hole)
When a slight noise he hears,
He pricks up his ears (two fingers go up on fisted hand)
And jumps into his hole in the ground. (two hands join)

Little Frog

This little frog broke his toe, (use index finger to touch fingers on other hand)
This little frog said, "Oh, oh, oh,"
This little frog cried and was sad,
This little frog laughed and was glad,
This little frog did just as he should,
And ran to his mother (or doctor) as fast as he could.

The Whole Family

This is the father, full of good cheer. (thumb)
This is the mother, kind and dear. (index finger)
This is the brother, strong and tall. (middle finger)
This is the sister, who plays with her doll. (ring finger)
This is the baby, the pet of all. (small finger)
This is the family, great and small.

The Farm

Ten little children (hold up ten fingers)
On a farm one day,
Ran in the meadow (make fingers run)
And jumped in the hay, (make fingers leap)
Drove all the horses (hold reins)
To the big hay mow,
And ran to the pasture (make fingers run)
Where they milked a cow. (motions of milking)

My Haircut

The clippers go clip, (run fingers up neck)
And the scissors go snip, (work two fingers like scissors)
And the hair falls down in my lap. (wiggle fingers from head to lap)
The brush goes swish once or twice, (brush at neck)
I look in the mirror and I look nice!
(hold hands before face)

Two Houses

Two little houses all closed up tight! (fist closed, thumbs closed in)
Open up the window and let in the light. (fingers and thumbs stretched)
Ten little finger people, tall and straight, (palms to the front, fingers erect)
Ready for school at half past eight. (fingers erect, hands and arms move jerkily forward)

Ten Little Fingers

I have ten little fingers,
And they belong to me.
I can make them do things,
Would you like to see?

I can open them wide,
I can shut them up tight.
I can put them together,
I can put them out of sight.

I can put them up high,
I can put them down low.
I can fold them quietly,
And sit just so.

Five Little Squirrels

Five little squirrels sitting in a tree,
The first one said, "What do I see?" (hold up index finger)
The second one said, "A man with a gun." (add middle finger)
The third one said, "Let's run, lets run." (add ring finger)
The fourth one said, "Let's hide in the shade."(add little finger)
The fifth one said, "I'm not afraid." (add thumb)
When bang (clap) went the gun, and how they did run! (hide fingers behind back)

Two Little Dicky Birds

Two little dicky birds, (fingers closed, thumbs up)
Sitting on a hill,
One named Jack, (wiggle right thumb)
One named Jill. (wiggle left thumb)
Fly away Jack, (swing right hand around to back)
Fly away, Jill, (swing left hand around to back)
Come back, Jack, (return right hand with thumb up)
Come back, Jill. (return left hand with thumb up)

Mousie Brown

He climbed up the candle stick,
The little mousie brown,
To steal and eat some tallow,
But he couldn't get down.
He called for his grandma,
But his grandma was in town,
So he doubled up into a wheel,
And rolled himself down.

The Little Spider

Little spider likes to climb up a window sill.
Up and up and up he goes,
Up and up until... (as left arm is held upright, fingers of right hand climb up arm)
He stands upon the very top, (fingers of right hand pause on tip of left hand)
Then down his web he slides. (fingers of right hand slide down left arm)
I think it must be lots of fun
To go on cobweb rides.

Mr. Bear

Here is a cave, (fingers bent)
Inside is a bear. (thumb inside fingers)
Now he comes out
To get some fresh air. (thumb out)
He stays out all summer
In sunshine and heat,
He hunts in the forest
For berries to eat. (thumb moving around in circle)

When snow starts to fall,
He hurries inside
His warm little cave
And there he will hide. (thumb inside fingers)
Snow covers the cave
Like a fluffy white rug. (fingers spread out of other hand)
Inside the bear sleeps
All cozy and snug. (one hand over other)

Pig Fun

Two mother pigs lived in a pen, (hold up thumbs)
Each had four babies and that made ten. (thumbs and fingers)
These four babies were black as night. (four fingers up)
These four babies were black and white. (other four fingers)

Now all eight babies loved to play, (wiggle fingers)
And they rolled and rolled in the mud each day.
And at night with their mothers, they curled in a heap,
And squealed and squealed till they went to sleep.

Mr. Left and Mr. Right

This is Mr. Left. (left thumb)
This is Mr. Right. (right thumb)
They have two little houses just alike. (two fists)
Mr. Left says, "Hi there, how are you tonight?"(wave left thumb)
Mr. Right says, "Hello, I'm all right!" (wave right thumb)
So arm in arm, off they go. (hook thumbs)
They talk and they walk, first fast, then slow.
Back they come, wave goodnight,
Pop into their houses and out of sight. (teacher reverses hands when she faces children)

Five Little Ants

When I saw an ant hill (right hand with thumb clasped)
With no ants about,
I said, "Little ants,
Won't you please come out?"
Then, as if they had heard my call
One, two, three, four, five came out (lift each finger)
And that was all.

The Wind

Leaves are floating down, (open hands flutter down)
They make a carpet on the ground.
When, swish! The wind comes whirling by (hands move quickly to the side like wind blowing)
And sends them dancing to the sky. (hands fly up)

Five Little Jack o' Lanterns

Five little jack-o-lanterns sitting on a gate (hold up fingers and thumb)
The first one said, "My, it's getting late."
(touch each finger with other index finger as fingers are counted)
The second one said, "Who goes there?"
The third one said, "There are ghosts in the air."
The fourth one said, "Come, let's run."
The fifth one said, "It's only Halloween fun."
Puff came the wind, out went the lights (cup hands around mouth, and then move hands sideways like blowing wind)
Away ran the jack-o-lanterns on Halloween night. (hand behind back)

Thanksgiving Dinner

Here's a pumpkin for the pie, (show with both arms rounded)
Apples red to bake, (two fists)
Turkey for the roasting pan, (one fist with thumb as head, other hand makes tail)
I can hardly wait. (fold hands in lap)

Santa and His Reindeer

Eight tiny reindeer, prancing in the snow, (dance eight fingers with thumbs concealed)
Two chubby elf-men called out, "Whoa!" (bring out thumbs and pull them back)
Santa came out with a pack on his back, (put imaginary pack over shoulder)
And a whip in his hand that snapped (snap fingers)
With a crack. (clap hands)
He called to his elf-men (put hands to mouth)
And whistled in glee. (whistle)
Then he jumped in his sled (jump up hands)
And gave a big sigh, (sigh)
And away they went skimming through the sky. (make fingers fly)

Winter

What does the hail say? (pound fists three times)
What does the rain say? (Tap, tap, tap,)
What does the sleet say? (Lightly tap)
What does the wind say? (oo-oo-oo)
What does the snow say? (Fingers go down)

Abraham Lincoln

Lincoln hoed the growing corn, (hoe)
Chopped the family's wood, (chop)
Built a cabin out of logs, (pound)
Read all the books he could. (read)

Activity Poems

Activity poems have more body movement than fingerplays; the movements are self-evident in each poem. After you've taught the poem, choose different children to lead the activity—another chance for them to experience success.

The Traffic

I can run, run, run,
I can hop, hop, hop.
When I see a red light,
I must stop, stop, stop.

Whirly, Twirly

Like a leaf or a feather
In the windy windy weather,
We will whirl around and twirl around
And all sit down together.

Jack-in-the-Box

Jack-in-the-box, all shut up tight,
Not a breath of air, not a peep of light.
How tired he must be, all in a hump,
Open the lid and out he'll jump.

Rag Doll

Play you're my rag doll, don't make a sound!
Fling your arms and body round and round.
Fling your hands, fling your feet,
Let your head go free—
Be the raggedest rag doll
You ever did see.

Stretching

I reach for the sky,
I touch my eyes,
I reach for my toes,
I pinch my nose.

Ride Your Bike

Pedal your bicycle (make fists pedal slow)
Up the hill
Slow, slow, slow!
Turn around and down again
As fast as you can go. (make fists pedal fast)
(Option: lay on back, use legs to pedal)

Moving

Here we go up, up, up,
And here we go down, down, down,
Here we go backwards and forwards,
And here we go around, around, around.

I Wish . . .

I wish I were a jumping Jack,
I'd jump up from a box.
I wish I were a rocking horse,
I'd rock and rock and rock.
I wish I were a spinning top,
I'd spin around and 'round.
But I am just a little child
Who sits right down.

Johnny Works with One Hammer

Johnny works with one hammer, (fist "hammers" knee)
One hammer, one hammer,
Johnny works with one hammer,
Then he works with two.

Johnny works with two hammers, (two fists)
Two hammers, two hammers,
Johnny works with two hammers,
Then he works with three.

Johnny works with three hammers, (two fists and one foot tapping the floor)
Three hammers, three hammers,
Johnny works with three hammers,
Then he works with four.

Johnny works with four hammers, (two fists and two feet)
Four hammers, four hammers,
Johnny works with four hammers,
Then he works with five.

Johnny works with five hammers, (fists, feet, and add head)
Five hammers, five hammers,
Johnny works with five hammers,
Then he goes to sleep. (nod head)

Quiet Walk

Tippy, tippy, tip-toe
Here we go,
Tippy, tippy, tip-toe
To and fro.
Tippy, tippy, tip-toe
Through the house,
Tippy, tippy, tip-toe
Quiet as a mouse.

Getting the Wiggles Out

We rap, rap, rap
We clap, clap, clap
And we fold our arms just so.
And we look to the right and we look to the left,
And we nod our heads just so!

We stand up high, spread our arms so wide
And we whirl around just so!
And we point like this (right toe)
And we point like that (left toe)
And we all sit down just so!
(If teacher is facing children, when she says left,
she does right, etc.)

Blast Off

(Sit with elbows close to the body and hands held in front,
with tips of fingers touching to form cone of a rocket.)
Inside a rocket ship,
Just enough room.
Here comes the countdown —
10, 9, 8, 7, 6, 5, 4, 3, 2, 1, 0,
Ignition, blast off and
Zoo-o-o-o-o-m!
(Stand up and raise arms as high as possible with fingers still held together like the cone of a rocket.)

The Floppy Scarecrow

Flip flop, flip flop,
See the scarecrow go —
Flip flop, flip flop,
Bending to and fro.
To the left, to the right,
Back and forth with all his might.
Then the wind is quiet and so —
Flip flop, flop (slowly)
Flip flop, flop, FLOP! (very slowly)

Scarecrow

Scarecrow, scarecrow, turn around,
Scarecrow, scarecrow, jump up and down,
Scarecrow, scarecrow, wink one eye.
Scarecrow, scarecrow, bend your knees,
Scarecrow, scarecrow, flop in the breeze,
Scarecrow, scarecrow, climb into bed.
Scarecrow, scarecrow, rest your head.

Head, Shoulders, Knees, Toes

Head, shoulders, knees, toes,
Head, shoulders, knees, toes,
Head shoulders, knees, toes,
We all stand up together.

Head, shoulders, knees, toes,
Head, shoulders, knees, toes,
Head, shoulders, knees, toes,
We all sit down together.

Teddy Bear, Teddy Bear

Teddy Bear, Teddy Bear, turn around,
Teddy Bear, Teddy Bear, touch the ground.
Teddy Bear, Teddy Bear, tap your toes,
Teddy Bear, Teddy Bear, pinch your nose.
Teddy Bear, Teddy Bear, turn around,
Teddy Bear, Teddy Bear, please sit down.

Ten Little Indian Boys

One little, two little, three little Indians, (use fingers)
Four little, five little, six little Indians,
Seven little, eight little, nine little Indians,
Ten little Indian boys.

Each one rode a spotted pony, (repeat 3 times and make riding motion)
Ten little . .
Each one did an Indian war dance, (etc.)
Ten little . . .
Each one shot a big fat turkey, (etc.)
Ten little . . .
Each one paddled a little canoe, (etc.)
Wet little Indian boys. (fall backwards in water)
(Can be used as a circle game—add a child as number
is called—activity in center of circle.)

Crafts

Crafts are one of the self-selected activities available during worktime. Particular projects will often be related to the unit theme; many require preparation which should be completed before worktime begins. If an aide is not available, recruit parent volunteers to help with these tasks. Using parents may take extra time in the beginning, but with proper training they can save you time and effort.

When introducing a new craft, gather materials and make the item while explaining the procedure to the children. Include the most simple details—do not assume they know how to do any of it. Following this procedure will help the child accomplish the task with less frustration and save you from repeating the same explanation over and over.

The craft suggestions are arranged according to the school year—fall, Halloween, Thanksgiving, etc. The last few pages include ideas and "recipes" which can be used at any time.

The following list of crafts is in the same order in which they appear in the text.

SCRIBBLE DRAWING
SHAPES
PICKER STICKERS
TRAFFIC LIGHT

SCHOOL BUS
HEIGHT CHART
DRAW AROUND THE CHILD
NUTRITION; FOOD GROUPS
HOBGOBLINS
SACK MASKS
PLASTIC MASKS
PAPER PLATE MASKS
TRICK OR TREAT SACK
FALL LEAVES
TOTEM POLES
HEAD BANDS
INDIAN DRUMS
WIGWAMS
INDIAN WITH BLANKETS
POTTERY
TURKEYS
WINTER
BIRD FEEDER
CHRISTMAS ORNAMENT
BELLS
HAND PRINTS
CANDY CANE
POPCORN TREE
WRAPPING PAPER
STAR OF DAVID
GREETING CARDS
SANTA
JANUARY CALENDAR
CLOCKS
SNOW
WHERE WE LIVE
HEALTH AND SAFETY AT HOME
THE DOCTOR
DENTIST
FIREMAN HAT
POLICE BADGE
FINGERPRINTS
POSTAL WORKER
VALENTINES
VALENTINE MAN

VALENTINE TREE
WASHINGTON'S THREE-CORNERED HAT
FLAG
LOG CABINS
RED, WHITE, AND BLUE COLLAGE
KITES
PIN WHEELS
SAILBOAT
TREES
EASTER HATS
STAINED GLASS WINDOWS
EASTER CARDS
EASTER BASKET
BUNNY EARS
SPACE SHIPS
SPACE HELMETS
ROCKETS
BINOCULARS
FLYING SAUCER
BUTTON FLOWERS
TULIP
PUSSY WILLOW
BIRD HOUSE
BIRD CAGE
FLOWER OR MAY BASKETS
VASE
CATERPILLAR
BUTTERFLIES
TURTLE
SNAKE
SHOPPING CENTER
CIRCUS CLOWN
ZOO ANIMALS
FINGER PAINTING
BLOCK PRINTING
DRIP PAINTING
CHALK PAINTING
STRING PAINTING
SANDPAPER PICTURES
EXTENSION PHONES
PAPERWEIGHTS

STRAW PAINT PICTURES
BOTTLE PAINTING
CRAYON ETCHING
SAWDUST MODELING
CREATIVE CRAFT DOUGH
PLAY DOUGH

Scribble Drawing

Have child scribble a design and fill in areas with different colors.

Shapes

Have patterns for children to trace and cut (if children are ready for scissors). Have some shapes pre-cut for children to use in making a collage by pasting designs on paper.

Picker Stickers

Children pick items from boxes of buttons, lace, scraps of cloth, pieces of wallpaper, seeds, etc. and paste them on a piece of construction paper to make a collage. (This craft can come and go. Later in the year, children might decorate rooms in a house they have drawn or use pieces of cloth for a lady's dress, etc.)

Traffic Light

Place three-inch squares of red, orange and green paper on a craft table. Have children round off corners and paste on a shoe box, cereal box, or a piece of construction paper.

School Bus

Make a school bus from a milk carton, using plastic lids for wheels. Cover carton with paper or color. Cut out windows and attach wheels with fasteners.

Height Chart

Measure children, record on chart and post in room (this is a good activity to repeat after the holidays and at the end of the year). If you have wall space, use adding machine tape for each child's height. Write child's name on tape. Later you can add growth to same graph.

Draw Around the Child

Have child lie on butcher paper. Trace around child. Child cuts out form and colors it (fun to put in hall).

Nutrition—Food Groups

Divide paper into four. Have children cut and paste from each of four food groups (bread and cereal, fruit and vegetable, dairy products, and meat).

Or, as a class project, children use cut-out pictures from home or magazines at school to make health charts on easel paper or tag board.

Hobgoblins

Use black and orange construction paper.

Cut and paste:

body - 4" x 5"; arm - 1" x 4"

head - 2-1/2" x 2-1/2"; leg 1" x 9"

Fold legs and arms back and forth "like a fan." Makes them wiggle.

Black spiders can be made the same way.

Sack Masks
Use brown paper sacks that will fit down over the child's face. Children use their own creative ideas as to design and type of face.

Plastic Masks
Gallon milk bottles are used. Remove bottom of bottle and cut top to shape of mask desired. Then slit the bottle down one side and punch holes for strings to fasten mask to head. Cut eye, nose, and mouth holes. Decorate.

Paper Plate Masks
Cut eye, nose, and mouth holes. Decorate and punch holes for strings to fasten mask to head.

Trick or Treat Sacks
Make from large brown grocery sacks. Print "Trick or Treat" on one side of sack. Children decorate the sack as they please. Fold down top of sack for strength. Punch two holes through both sides of top. Run heavy cord through holes and tie. Children can do all of this for themselves.

Fall Leaves
1. Trace around hand (fingers can be together or spread apart) on different colored construction paper (use color of fall leaves). Cut out and place on "tree trunk." This is good for bulletin boards.
2. Cut shavings from crayons and place between two pieces of wax paper. Press with warm iron and cut into leaf shapes.
3. Crayon Rubbing: Place paper over leaf and color.
4. Finger Paint Print: Put finger paint on back of leaf, turn leaf, place back side down carefully on sheet of paper. Cover with a newspaper and press carefully; remove top newspaper and leaf.
5. Make leaf people by gluing a leaf on a piece of construction paper and coloring arms, legs, and head.

Totem Poles
1. Use a towel roll, bits of colored paper and crayons. Popsicle sticks may be added as wings.
2. Use empty thread spools. Color or paint faces (human or animal) on each spool. Then glue spools together. Cut noses, eyes, ears, bills, wings, feet, etc. from construction paper and paste on.

Head Bands
Cut 4" strips from large brown grocery sacks, fold in half, and decorate with Indian motifs. Cut feathers freehand from 2" x 9" strips of construction paper (color feathering or clip in on each side). Paste feathers in between the folded band and staple to fit individual child's head.

Indian Drums
Paint or color designs on round boxes. Use stick (from tree) for drum stick; cover end with stuffed cloth and tie with yarn.

Wigwams
Use 9" x 12" stiff brown wrapping paper and cut into cone shape. Decorate with Indian designs. Fasten with toothpicks.

Indians with Blankets
Use construction paper.
Head: 4" x 2-1/2", make head with long neck.
Blanket: 6" x 9", decorate and then fold around neck (cone shape).
Feather: 1" x 1-1/2", shape to point.

Pottery
Use bottom third of a quart size bleach bottle. For papier-mache covering, apply 1" wide strips of newspaper alternately with wallpaper paste, adding several layers to achieve the shape and appearance desired. Allow to dry and then paint entire piece with desired basic color(s). After paint is dry, add painted Indian designs in contrasting colors.

Turkeys
1. Paper plate turkey: cut head and neck from brown construction paper; paste on edge of paper plate. Make wattle red and eye black. Color feathers in circular pattern around plate.
2. Paper sack turkey: stuff small brown paper sack 1/2 full and tie. Cut top of bag in strips for tail. Make head from construction paper. Color feathers.
3. Trace around hand for turkey shape (head is thumb and fingers are tail feathers) on construction paper. Add legs and background. Color.

Winter
"Homework": Cut out pictures of clothes we wear in winter. Pin on bulletin board, paste in a booklet, or make a chart.

Bird Feeder
1. Fill pine cone with peanut butter, roll in bird seed.
2. Form ground suet into a ball. Wrap with large plastic netting used for fruit sacks.
3. Hang from tree.

Christmas Ornament
Glue sequins and glitter on pine cones.

Bells
1. Cut foil tart shells to center; form a bell. Staple ribbon to top.
2. Make bells out of egg cartons, trim or paint.

Hand Prints
1. Make splatter prints of children's hands on construction paper.
2. Make plaster of Paris hand prints.

Candy Cane
On a 8" x 8" square of white paper, color a 1/2" red strip along two adjacent edges. Turn the paper over and start rolling a pencil from the corner that is not red. Tape the end piece. Remove pencil and curl one end of the paper cylinder around the pencil, forming the curved end of the candy cane.

Popcorn Tree
Drop popped corn into bags containing small amounts of powdered tempera paint. Shake the bags. Glue the colored corn on a tree shape for ornaments.

Wrapping Paper
Cut sponge or potato in Christmas or Hanukkah shapes. Use for stenciling wrapping paper.

Star of David
Use two gold triangles to make the Star of David. Paste triangles on a blue field.

Greeting Cards
1. Frosted Cards: To create frost crystals, add Epsom salts to warm water, stirring constantly until no more crystals will dissolve. This solution, when painted on paper and dried, will create sparkling crystals.

2. Pictures: Glue a colored picture from magazine or old greeting card to a piece of cardboard the same size. Dilute white glue with equal amount of water. Cover all or part of picture with glue; when dry, apply Epsom salt solution with a brush. You may cover the whole picture, only the background, or certain details, such as trees or roof tops. When dry, glue to folded construction paper. Add message.
3. Rubbings: Cut small cardboard designs such as stars, candles, etc. Place design between folds of construction paper. Rub the side of the crayon across the construction paper and the designs will appear. Fold and add message.

Santa

Follow instructions for Halloween hobgoblins, but use red and white paper.

January Calendar

Have stark calendar for month ready; children put numerals in appropriate places.

Clocks

1. Make clocks from paper plates, with numerals drawn around outside. Hands are cut from black construction paper and attached with a fastener, so they move.
2. Make wrist watch from ice cream container lid. Put on face, punch holes, and use yarn to tie around wrist.

Snow

1. Cut snowflakes from 6" paper squares that have been folded. Tape to window.
2. Whipped soap snow: beat equal amounts of Ivory Snow soap and water to form a very stiff substance. Child drops some on a plastic lid, stands up a small picture cut from old Christmas card, sprinkles with glitter and lets dry overnight.
3. Glue popped corn on dark blue paper for snow scenes.

Where We Live

1. Paint shoe boxes for houses, apartments from large boxes. Make windows, doors, and roofs out of construction paper.
2. Fold large news print in four sections; unfold and lines represent room divisions. Children color each room like a room in their home.

Health and Safety at Home

Teach:"Whenever you have to cough or sneeze,
Remember to cover your mouth up, please."
Children paste a copy of poem on construction paper and draw a picture of someone sneezing.

The Doctor

Make doctor's head mirror by cutting circle from cardboard, cover with foil, and staple to white wrapping paper headband.

Dentist

1. Same as doctor.
2. Lost tooth club: cut large white poster board in shape of tooth. When children loose a tooth, they sign their name.

Fireman Hat

Take one full sheet of newsprint, painted red, and fold in one half. Fold in half again; open this up and fold top corners in diagonal to center crease line. Turn up bottom edge on each side and staple; fold front up and staple.

Police Badge

Cover star with foil. Use double stick tape to wear.

Fingerprints

Make fingerprints with ink pad. Use magnifying glass to see how different they are.

Postal Worker

Hat: cut and color a paper sack.

Mail Bag: fold down top of large brown paper bag three times to form a band. Make shoulder strap by cutting a strip of brown paper and staple to bag. Make letters to fill bag.

Valentines

1. Make book-type valentines by folding construction paper into four sections. Decorate with scraps of different colored construction paper and/or color. Add message.
2. Doily prints: Glue several unseparated heart-shaped doilies to the underside of a paper plate. Brush paint across the doilies and invert on the paper to be printed. Rub the plate lightly; two or three prints can be made from one inking.
3. Glue a cut-out in the center of a doily, mount on construction paper, and add a message.

Valentine Man

Cut a 4" heart for body and a 3" heart for head. Use 1" x 9" strips for legs and 1" x 6" strips for arms (accordion folded). Paste legs and arms on body, draw a face; attach a piece of yarn at the top.

Valentine Tree

Mix plaster of Paris and pour in plastic container. Place a tree twig in center and let dry. Children cut red, pink, and white hearts, and either glue them on tree or attach yarn to them and hang. This can be done individually using paper cups and smaller twigs.

Washington's Three-cornered Hat

Take one full sheet of newsprint and fold in one half. Fold in half again; open last fold and fold top corners in diagonal to center crease line. Turn up bottom edge on each side and staple. Children decorate.

Flag (a class project)

1. Make red and white paper chains from construction paper. Pin on bulletin board for stripes. Pin blue construction paper for field and thirteen stars can be colored with chalk.
2. Paste 3 long red stripes (12" x 1/2"), 4 short red strips (6" x 1/2") on white paper. Paste blue field (6" x 4-1/2"). Use chalk or silver stars.

Log Cabins

1. Use corrugated paper, cut out cabin shape and mount on construction paper. Color windows, doors and scenery.
2. Glue pretzels on paper in shape of a cabin.

Red, White, and Blue Collage

Have many sizes, shapes, designs and textures, (construction paper, cloth, wallpaper, etc.) in the three colors. Also have available stickers—flags, stars, bells, etc. Children make collage on 9" x 12" background paper.

Kites

Cut corners off a 9" x 12" piece of construction paper to form a diamond shape. Decorate, add yarn for tail and attach small scraps of paper on the tail.

Pin Wheels

Fold a 6" square of paper diagonally, both ways. Paper folds will form an "X." Cut on each fold to within one inch of center. Stick a straight pin through every other point, the center of the paper and into the eraser end of a pencil or the end of a small stick.

Sailboat

Use round plastic tub for hull. Cut small hole and insert pencil for mast. Make sail from piece of paper. Punch a hole at the top and bottom of the sail and slide pencil through. Add enough sand to the bottom so that it maintains balance in the water.

Trees

1. On construction paper, draw a tree trunk. Glue small squares of red tissue paper for a red bud flower.
2. Use popped corn for an apple tree.

Easter Hats

Decorate paper plates using crayons, scraps of paper, fabric, etc. Add crepe paper streamers to tie under chin.

Stained Glass Windows

Shave crayons (several colors) onto wax paper. Cover with another piece of wax paper and press with warm iron. Fold 9" x 12" piece of construction paper and cut out center leaving a 1" frame when unfolded. Staple wax paper to back.

Easter Cards

Fold paper into card shape. Make bunny using three cotton balls with construction paper ears (make ears wide and fold for a dimensional effect). Add verse.

Easter Basket

Start with a sturdy container—the bottom of a plastic jug is good. Line with an 18" piece of plastic. Fill with 2" of soil, then plant rye grass in basket. Tie the plastic over both soil and seeds to create a greenhouse (it takes two weeks for the seed to grow). Untie and trim plastic after seeds have sprouted. Makes attractive grass for eggs.

Bunny Ears

Cut two ear shapes from 12"x 18" white construction paper. Paint or color middle of ears pink. Fold easel paper to make a headband. Slide ears in between folds of headband and staple in place. Fit headband to child's head and staple.

Space Ships

1. On dark blue paper, paste rocket made from 6" x 1-1/2" rectangle with top corners cut into a point. Use yellow circle for moon and red scrap for rocket exhaust. Add silver stars or draw stars with chalk.
2. Provide many different shapes such as rectangles and triangles, and let children create their own designs.

Space Helmets

1. Gallon plastic milk or water jugs can be cut to shape.
2. Use paper sacks decorated with paper cups, wire, electric cord, pipe cleaners, etc.

Rockets

Use cardboard tubes, add nose cone (make from circle of construction paper; cut to center, overlap edges and glue or staple). Slit sides to put in cardboard fins.

Binoculars

Fasten two toilet paper rolls together.

Flying Saucer

Staple two small foil plates together and write numeral on top. Make faces of spacemen to insert into saucer.

Button Flowers

Use buttons as center of construction paper flowers. Either color petals or cut and paste them.

Tulip

Cut egg cartons and paint as flowers; use pipe cleaner for stem.

Pussy Willow

Using 9" x 12" construction paper, draw and color a branch, or glue on real limb. Add bits of cotton for "pussy willows."

Bird House

Obtain half-gallon milk cartons and paint them. Take construction paper, 6" x 7" and fold in middle; staple to peaked top of carton to make the roof. About halfway down on the side of the carton, cut a hole 2" in diameter.

Bird Cage

Tie two plastic strawberry cartons together with colored yarn. Children draw a bird on oak tag, cut out and paste on paper limb. Paste limb and bird inside cage, then hang in window.

Flower or May Baskets

1. Use plastic strawberry carton with pipe cleaner handle. Children make flowers by cutting and pasting from colored paper.
2. Remove top of 1/2 pint milk carton. Cover with construction or contact paper, and add handle made of yarn or pipe cleaner.
3. Fold a square of vinyl wallpaper diagonally into two triangles. Staple a strip of wallpaper to top corners for handle.

Vase

Cut off top of any type or size of liquid detergent bottle. Glue on bits of rick-rack, felt, lace, glitter, etc.

Caterpillar

Form circles by pasting together ends of 6" x 1" paper strips, but do not interlock links. Glue them to each other on outside, then add paper eyes and antennas.

Butterflies

1. Gather 8" squares of pastel tissue in middle and insert in clothespin. Add pipe cleaners for antenna and draw eyes with marking pen.
2. Draw around child's shoes, feet close together. Cut out and color.

3. Pre-cut and fold butterfly shapes. Drop paint on one side, fold and press for symmetrical design. Glue plastic spoon in middle for body.

Turtle

Color two paper plates for top and bottom of body. Cut feet, tail, and head from construction paper; paste to edges of plates. Staple plates together.

Snake

Cut a paper plate into a spiral (start at outside edge for tail and head will be in the center). Color design on both sides, add eyes. Stretch out snake to stand.

Shopping Center

Make shops out of shoe boxes; put together for a center. Color and name shops.

Circus Clown

Cover cardboard tube with white paper (toilet paper is good size). Color on face. Use yarn or paper strips for hair. Make cone-shaped hat and paper ruffle around bottom.

Zoo Animals

1. Color animal on 9" x 12" manila paper, put brown 2" strip at top and bottom. Add wheels and bars (straws).
2. Color animal on meat tray. Sew yarn bars.
3. Color animal on meat tray and then sew around the animal shape.

Finger Painting

1. Finger paint on cookie sheet, then lay paper on top. Design comes off on paper.
2. Finger paint using instant pudding. Make sure children have clean hands so they can "taste" the paint.

Block Printing

Use spools, corks, pencils, potato designs (cut potato in half and cut design such as star, tree, etc.), sponge, etc. Make printing pad by stapling several pieces of felt together, saturate with water first, then with desired color. Then press item against pad and on construction paper or newsprint.

Drip Painting

Put a few drops of paint near fold of paper; press fold with fingers and across the paper to the outer edge. Open paper to see picture.

Chalk Painting

Wet a paper towel with water or buttermilk. Draw with colored chalk and dry.

String Painting

Lay string that has been dipped in tempera between folded paper and press.

Sandpaper Pictures

Color with crayon on sandpaper.

Extension Phones

Poke a hole in the bottom of two tin cans. Use length of string, bring to inside of each can and knot. Have children talk to each other through cans.

Paperweights

Paint rocks using poster paint combined with Elmer's glue to make it adhere.

Straw Paint Pictures

Each child has a piece of finger paint paper and a straw. Drop from medicine dropper several drops of different colors of paint. Child blows through the straw to create patterns and designs.

Bottle Painting

1. Squeeze bottle filled with paint of heavy consistency. Make outline and then fill in. Let dry before using another color.
2. Fill a bottle with paint and wad a piece of wet sponge into the neck. Stamp sponge lightly on paper for patterns.
3. Roll-on bottles distribute paint as the ball revolves. Hold bottle as you would a pen, moving quickly and smoothly.
4. Pads: use liquid shoe polish bottles. Dab the pad into tempera or white shoe polish; make lines or polka dots.

Crayon Etching

Prepare paper for etching by applying a heavy coat of blue for sky, green for grass, and perhaps some red in one corner for a barn. Use a black crayon to darken entire paper. Scratch a design with a sharp object (nail) so that the color underneath shows.

Sawdust Modeling

This mixture looks like cork when dry and can be decorated with paint or glitter as well as sanded and shellacked. It can be sculpted, rolled out, or applied as a covering material. Mix four cups sawdust, 1/2 cup plaster of Paris, and 1-1/2 cups of dry wallpaper paste. Add water until mixture is like clay. To store overnight, cover with damp cloth. Set projects in well ventilated place to dry.

Projects:

a. Totem Pole: line cardboard roll with wax paper, fill roll, then pull off paper to remove the clay roll. Decorate.
b. Cover can with sawdust mixture. Use a fork to create bark-like texture.
c. Creative sculpting.

Creative Craft Dough

1 cup cornstarch 1/2 cup cold water
2 cups table salt
2/3 cup water
food coloring if desired, or may be painted when dry.

Stir together cornstarch and 1/2 cup cold water in bowl. Mix salt and 2/3 cup water in saucepan over low heat until quite warm. Stir cornstarch and cold water mixture into salt mixture. When quite warm and consistency of stiff dough, cool the mixture, remove from pan, and knead like dough. Items take 24 to 36 hours to dry.

Play Dough

2 cups flour
2 tablespoons salad oil
1 cup salt
food coloring or tempera

Add water slowly until the mixture is pliable. Knead ingredients and put in plastic bag. This will harden if not kept in plastic bag when not in use.

Games

All games which require that the children form a circle have the added value of helping children to orient themselves in space—a prerequisite to reading.

If you start a game, you have a chance to do some subtle ego-building by calling on a child who is not frequently chosen. Simple games that include all the children are the best.

For circle games, a child sits after having a turn.

Good Morning

Children form a circle. Teacher, in the center of the circle, says, "Good Morning, ______," and exchanges places with the child. That child comes to the center of the circle and says "Good Morning" to another child, then returns to the circle and sits. Procedure is repeated until all children have a turn.

Other phrases can be:

Have a nice day.

I'll see you tomorrow.

Happy Thanksgiving.

Merry Christmas.

This may seem inane, but don't underestimate its appeal. It is a good stand-up activity for transition, and the children enjoy it.

I Bounce the Ball

The teacher stands in the middle of the circle and bounces a large rubber ball as she says:

"I bounce the ball to _______."

The child whose name is called catches the ball. Then the child bounces it back to the teacher and says: "I bounce the ball to _______ (teacher's name)."

The teacher continues to call other names until each child has had a turn.

Hot Ball

Children sit in a circle with legs crossed. The ball is "hot" and must be pushed away when it comes near a child or she will be "burned."

Knock Down the Tower

Children sit in a circle around a small tower of blocks. A child rolls a ball to try and knock down the tower. When the tower falls, the successful child rebuilds the tower and then gives the ball to another child.

Color Ball

Two children stand in center of circle. Teacher pins a circle of red, yellow, green, blue, or orange on the back of one child. The other child moves about in an effort to see the color, which the first child tries to keep hidden. When the other child calls out the color (or when time is called), the two participants choose two more children.

Hickory, Dickory, Dock

Two children stand in the middle of the circle representing a clock and a mouse. They skip around inside the circle while the group says:

"Hickory, dickory, dock!
The mouse ran up the clock;
The clock struck _____
And down he ran,
Hickory, dickory, dock."

When the group says "the clock struck," the clock says, "How many times do you want the clock to strike, Mousie?" The mouse may answer any number from one to six. Then the children in the circle clap that number of times and call the number. Mouse and clock choose two other children and repeat.

Wee Willie Winkie

Five children sit in the middle of the circle with their heads down, as if asleep. A child chosen as Wee Willie Winkie runs around them as the group says:

"Wee Willie Winkie runs through the town,
Up stairs and down stairs in his nightgown,
Rapping at the windows, crying through the locks,
'Are the children in their beds? It is eight o'clock.'"

On the last line of the rhyme, Wee Willie Winkie touches the five children and they wake up.

Jack Be Nimble

Children are in circle formation. Two or three small blocks are stacked in the middle of the floor. Children say the rhyme:

"Jack be nimble,
Jack be quick,
Jack jump over
The candlestick."

On the word "jump" a child who has been chosen from the circle runs out and jumps over the blocks. Child's name may be substituted for "Jack."

Lollipops

One child skips around the circle with a box or basket of paper "lollipops." The group says "Lollipops! Lollipops! Who will buy my lollipops?" The child stops before another child and asks, "What color do you want?" If the child says, "Red," the one with the lollipops hands over a red one from the box and then continues around the circle until all of the colors are gone.

Little Miss Muffet
One girl, chosen to be "Miss Muffet," is seated in the middle of the circle with her back to another child, chosen to be the spider. The children chant the rhyme:
"Little Miss Muffet,
Sat on a tuffet,
Eating her curds and whey;
There came a big spider,
And sat down beside her,
And frightened Miss Muffet away."
When the words, "sat down beside her" are spoken, the spider runs over and sits down beside Miss Muffet, who jumps up and runs to her place in the circle.

I Spy a Bean Bag
Choose five children, who cover their eyes. Hide five bean bags around the room where those children can find them. At the signal, "Ready," these children walk to find the bean bags. When a bean bag is found, the player should say, "I spy a bean bag," and bring the bag to the circle. When all bean bags have been found, those who found them hide them again.

Squirrel in the Tree
The players separate into groups of three. One or two extra players are squirrels. Two children in each group face each other and join both hands with their arms held up, forming a tree. The third child, a squirrel, stands between the arms of the other two. At a signal from the teacher, all squirrels leave their trees and walk as fast as possible, trying to get into an empty tree. At this time the extra squirrels try to get into trees, too. When there is a squirrel in each tree, extra children become squirrels for the next game.

After several repetitions of the game, have the children change places. Instruct each squirrel to choose a child to exchange places with him. Before the game ends, make certain that everyone has had an opportunity to be a squirrel.

Hula Hoop and Bean Bags
Two children hold a hula hoop; the other children take turns trying to toss a bean bag through the hoop. As the year goes by, increase the distance.

Catch
Children can practice tossing and catching large sponges.

Scarf Fun
Collect scarves. (The lost and found is a good source.) Give scarves to the children and play music. Let the children move and wave scarves to music.

Choo Choo

Make numbered cards in the shape of ten train cars. Number one is the engine; ten is the caboose. Give cards to the children. The engine starts chugging, stops and adds child with card number two. They chug and pick up number three. Procedure continues until all ten cars are chugging together.

Skip Along

Children form a circle. One child skips inside the circle and at a signal (if using music, when the music stops) the child picks a partner. They skip until the signal. Each picks another partner and all four skip. Procedure continues until the entire class is skipping.

Come Skip Along

One child is chosen to start the game. When the music starts, the child skips around the inside of the circle. While skipping, the child stops in front of several children, bows to them and says, "Come along." When the music stops, the class counts the number of children chosen.

Skipping Stoop

Children skip, run, or trot in a circle to piano or record accompaniment. When music stops, they stoop. The last child down is eliminated. The game continues until two or three children remain in the circle.

Hop to the Numeral

Child hops to the center of the circle, takes a numeral (or letter), hops back to the circle and calls the name of the numeral (or letter).

Across the River

Two lines are drawn (or yarn can be used) to represent the banks of the river. The children run to the line and jump over the river. Anyone missing the jump and landing in the river is sent "home" to put on dry shoes and socks. Then he can re-enter the game. To increase the difficulty, move lines further apart.

Relay

Divide class into two lines. Give a block to the first child in each line. At a signal, he hands the block to the child in back of him. When the child at the end of the line receives the block, he goes to the head of the line and repeats the procedure.

Block Relay
Two chairs are placed at one end of the room, and two at the opposite end. Three blocks are placed on each of the two chairs at one end of the room. Two players stand by the two chairs. On a given signal, each child picks up a block and runs with it to the chair at the other end of the room. They then run back and repeat the process until all of the blocks have been transferred to the chairs at the opposite end of the room. The children then return and sit on the chairs which originally held the blocks. The first child to sit on a chair wins the game.

Open the Gate
Girls form two lines and arch with their hands. They chant
"Open the gates as high as the sky,
Let all the king's horses come galloping by."
The boys then gallop through the arch.
Reverse using "queen's horses."

Gathering Leaves
Large colored leaves with numerals on them are placed around the room, and a corresponding number of children are chosen to gather or find one leaf each. When all the leaves are gathered, each child tells the color and the numeral on his or her leaf.

Hunter
Children sit in circle. One child is chosen as the wolf. Three others are chosen as a rabbit, a chicken, and a turkey. They hide in various homes around the room. The wolf says, "I am looking for my dinner. I think I'll have a rabbit." The rabbit must run from his home to a spot in the circle before he is caught by the wolf. Each animal is called in like manner.

Taking Turns
The children stand in a circle and count off by twos. The teacher asks all of one number to sit down. At a given signal, those sitting down stand up, and those standing up, sit down. Continue to alternate groups.

The Postman
Have available a mail bag of envelopes, each of which has a numeral from one to ten on its back. Children stand in a circle. One child, acting as the postman, takes the bag of envelopes, gives each child an envelope and returns to his place. Each child then "mails" his letter, saying the numeral on the envelope as he drops it into the mailbox (cardboard box with slit). Repeat with a new postman.

The Fireman
(Good outside game)
All children are numbered from one to four, with one child named fire chief. All the children with the same number should be grouped together at one goal line. The fire chief stands on another goal line and calls, "Fire! Fire! Station 1." The group that is called runs to the opposite goal line and back.

Picture Cards

Two identical sets of cards with pictures of objects are made. The first card has one object, the next card has two objects, etc., up to six. The children are given one set of cards and the matching set is placed on the floor. Each child must find the card which has the same number of objects as his own. Variations: number cards, word cards.

Clapping and Counting

One child is given a card with a numeral from one to six on it (one to ten second semester). The child skips around the circle and stops before another child who must clap the number of times that matches the numeral on the card.

Another way to play the same game is to keep the numeral hidden from the card's holder, who holds the card behind him and stops before a child who claps the matching number of times. The child holding the card must then guess the numeral on his card.

Ball Game

Ten children are given paper balls with a number on each. (The balls may be made from colored construction paper). The child holding the ball with "number one" skips to the child with "number two." The child with ball "number two" skips to "number three," etc., until all children have skipped in sequence.

Fishing

Large fish are made from different colored construction paper. A numeral is written on each fish. A paper clip is fastened to the mouth of the fish. A small magnet is tied to the end of a string. The different colored fish are spread around the inside of a circle which is the "pond." A child is chosen to go fishing. The magnet will pick up a fish, and the child tells the numeral that is written on the fish he has caught. The numeral can represent the number of pounds the fish weighs.

Taxi Ride

Four large taxicabs are made in different colors with a different numeral on each. Four matching cards are made with the same color and numeral for each one of the taxicabs. Four children are chosen to be drivers, and the sixteen cards are passed out to other children in the group. The teacher says, "Will all the children who are going to ride in taxicab number one stand behind their driver?" When all are "loaded" in their cabs, music may be played as the children have a tip-toe run behind their driver in an imaginary ride.

Where Am I

Four children are in different parts of the room—north, south, east, and west. Each child has an instrument, such as a triangle or drum. A child with his eyes closed sits in the middle of the circle. When he hears a sound, he indicates the direction of the sound by pointing. He may name the instrument.

Number Rhythms

One set of large number cards and several sets of matching smaller number cards are made. The smaller sets are distributed to the children. The teacher puts one of the larger number cards in a prominent place, names the number, and invites all of the children with the matching number card to skip, gallop, etc., using a different rhythm for each number.

Variations:

1. All children wearing red are asked to skip, etc.
2. Letter cards are given to children; the teacher holds up "d" or "p", names the letter and asks the children to hop.

I Spy

Choose a few children to go into another room. While they are gone, the teacher or child places a colored object in a fairly conspicuous spot. At a given signal, the children come back to the room to look for the object. When a child sees the object, he says "I spy" and goes back to his place. The search continues until all have found the object.

The Clock

One child stands in the middle of the circle while another child stands behind him with a triangle. All the others say,

"Here I sit in my rocking chair
And rock and rock and rock (Children rock).
Here I sit in my rocking chair
And listen to my clock."

The child with the triangle rings any number, one to twelve, and asks "What time is it?" The child in the middle answers. Each child chooses a replacement. If there is a rocking chair available, use it.

What's Missing?

Children sit in a circle. In the center of the circle, place several articles pertaining to good grooming, such as a comb, wash cloth, toothbrush, soap bar, and nailbrush (articles can also be related to the unit being studied). While one child sits with closed eyes, another removes one of the articles. The child who is "it" tries to name the missing article.

The Policeman and the Lost Child

The children stand in a circle with one child (the policeman) in the middle. The teacher says, "I'm looking for a lost child. Have you seen him?" The policeman says, "What does the lost child look like?" The teacher then describes a child who is in the circle. When the policeman recognizes the child, he calls out the child's name.

Musical Ball

Players stand in a circle facing the center. A ball is given to one player. When the music begins, the ball is passed from player to player. When the music stops, the player who has the ball in his hands must sit down. The game continues until there is only one player left.

Skipping Game

Children stand in a circle while one child skips around saying, "Fiddle-dee-dee, fiddle-dee-dee. I'll touch you and you touch me." The child stops and touches another child, who must then skip after the child who is "it."

Turn Around

Children in single file walk, skip, slide, or gallop clockwise around the circle. When the teacher gives a signal, or the music stops, all turn around quickly and go in a counter-clockwise direction.

Walk the Number Line

Make a walk-on number line (use continuous length of paper or vinyl). Children take turns walking to a particular numeral from one to ten. Later the activity may be varied, e.g., the child may be asked to walk to five, then take four more steps.

Skipping Tag

Children stand in a circle with one hand outstretched, palm up. One child skips inside circle to any skipping music and touches a second child's hand. The second child starts skipping in the opposite direction. The two meet, grasp hands, and skip around each other for two or three rounds. The first child becomes part of the circle again and the second child proceeds as did the first.

Thimble Three

The child who is "it" skips around the room with a thimble on his finger. When the word "touch" is said, the child with the thimble touches another child on the shoulder with the thimble and then skips back around the circle to his place. Children say the following chant as the child skips:
"Thimble, thimble, thimble three.
The one I touch skips after me."

Walk on Tiles

Tiles are marked with numerals one to ten and spread on floor. Children may cross the "brook" if they know the numeral. For example, a child may be asked to jump over numeral five. Or one tile could be covered up and the children asked to name the missing number tile. Children can also put tiles in proper numerical order.

We'll All Walk a Mile

(Tune: The Farmer in the Dell)
"We'll all walk a mile, we'll all walk a mile,
We'll walk a mile, and rest awhile.
We're one mile from home.
We'll all walk a mile, we'll all walk a mile,
We'll walk a mile, and rest awhile.
We're two miles from home."

This game may be varied by using "skip," "run," or "hop."

Repeat the above verse for about five or six miles as the children walk around the room in a line formation. When the word "awhile" is sung, stop each time and let the children tell how many miles from home they have walked. Reverse the line at the end of five or six miles and walk back, letting the children tell how many miles are left to be walked. Continue until last verse:

"We'll all walk a mile, we'll all walk a mile,
We'll walk a mile and rest awhile.
We're all back home."

Gobble! Gobble!

Three children close their eyes while three "turkeys" hide in the room. When a signal is given, the three children try to find the turkeys. While they are hunting, the turkeys say, "Gobble, gobble," until they are found.

Gathering Pumpkins

Large pumpkins with numerals on them are arranged on the floor to represent a field of pumpkins. Children take turns tossing bean bag on pumpkins. When bag lands on a pumpkin, child reads numeral, which tells how much the pumpkin weighs.

Santa Claus and Reindeer

Children are seated in a circle. Count off ten children to stand. The first is "Rudolph," who leads the way. The last is Santa, who drives the eight reindeer—children who stand in couples holding hands. Their outside hands hold the reins (yarn or ribbon). Rudolph holds both reins in one hand and rings a bell with the other. Santa "drives" while the children gallop to the tune of "Jingle Bells."

Bean Bag Toss

Draw a Christmas tree on the floor, divide it into sections, (masking tape can be used) and number each section. A child stands behind a line and throws at the tree. He must call the number in which the bean bag falls.

Santa's Reindeer

Five children are chosen to hide. Each has a jingle bell in his hand. A Santa is chosen who calls, "Where are my reindeer?" The reindeer must jingle their bells until Santa finds them.

Christmas Card Fun

Pass a Christmas card around the circle. When the triangle rings, or the music stops, the child holding the Christmas card gives it to the next child and sits down. Continue.
Variations: Valentine, Easter egg.

Be My Valentine

A "mailman" walks around the circle and stops before another child, asking "Will you be my Valentine?" They skip around the circle together, then the one chosen repeats the process.

Who Has the Valentine?

The children sit in a circle and one child leaves the room. Another child in the circle is given the valentine and sits on it. The child outside the room returns and asks, "______, do you have the valentine?" The child asked replies, "Yes, I have the valentine," or "No, I do not have the valentine." After two guesses the child says, "Who has the valentine?" The one who has it leaves the room and the game continues.
Variations: Christmas card, Easter egg.

Bunny, Bunny

A child is chosen to be a bunny. A rabbit ear hat made from construction paper is put on child's head. He hops to another child in the circle and says, "Bunny, bunny, how is your neighbor?" The child replies, "I don't know, but I'll go see." He puts on the hat and hops to another child in the circle. The game is repeated as before. "Hopping music" may be played during this game.

Mrs. Hen and Her Chicks

One child is chosen from the group to be Mrs. Hen, and five children are chosen to be her chicks. The mother hen goes to sleep, and the babies run and hide. She opens her eyes, sees that they are gone, and asks "Where are my babies?" The babies answer by saying, "Peep, peep." She follows the sound and brings them back to the circle. She counts to see if she has found them all.
Variation: Mrs. Hen goes to sleep. Teacher may touch five children or use name cards to choose chicks. All children sit in a circle and hide heads in their arms. Children chosen to be chicks say, "Peep, peep." Mother hen walks around circle trying to locate her chicks.

Bibliography

Developmental Theory and Research

Ames, Louise Bates, and Joan Ames Chase. *Don't Push Your Preschooler.* rev. ed. New York: Harper and Row, 1980.

Bruner, J. *The Process of Education.* Cambridge, MA: Harvard University Press, 1960.

Elkind, David. *The Hurried Child: Growing Up Too Fast Too Soon.* Reading, MA: Addison-Wesley, 1981.

Foster, Josephine C., and Neith E. Headley. *Education in the Kindergarten.* New York: American Book Co., 1948.

Hymes, James L. *Teaching the Child Under Six.* 3rd ed. Columbus, OH: Charles E. Merrill, 1981.

Ilg, Frances L., Louise Bates Ames, and Sidney M. Baker. *Child Behavior.* rev. ed. New York: Harper and Row, 1981.

Ilg, Frances L., Louise Bates Ames, and Jacqueline Haines. *School Readiness.* rev. ed. New York: Harper and Row, 1978.

Moore, Raymond S., and Dorothy N. Moore. *Better Late Than Early.* New York: Readers Digest Press, 1975.

Piaget, Jean. *Origins of Intelligence in Children.* Madison, CT: International University Press, 1966.

Sheldon, William. *Varieties of Temperment.* New York: Harper, 1942.

Singer, Dorothy G., and Tracey A. Revenson. *A Piaget Primer: How A Child Thinks.* New York: New American Library, 1978.

Wadsworth, Barry J. *Piaget for the Classroom Teacher.* New York: Longman, 1978.

Wadsworth, Barry J. *Piaget's Theory of Cognitive Development.* New York: Longman, 1979.

Developmental Curriculum

Ashton-Warner, Sylvia. *Teacher.* New York: Bantam, 1971.

Carll, Barbara, and Nancy Richard. *One Piece of the Puzzle: A Practical Guide for Schools Interested in Implementing a School Readiness Program.* Moravia, NY: Athena Publications, 1977.

Gardendale Elementary School. *Guidelines to the Developmental Kindergarten.* Brevard County School Board: Rockledge, FL, 1981.

Writing, Spelling, and Reading

Bissex, Glenda L. *Gnys at Wrk, A Child Learns to Write and Read.* Cambridge: Harvard University Press, 1980.

Calkins, Lucy McCormick. *The Art of Teaching Writing.* Portsmouth, NH: Heinemann, 1986.

Cullinan, Bernice. *Children's Literature in the Reading Program.* Portsmouth, NH: Heinemann, 1987.

Graves, Donald H. *Writing: Teachers and Children at Work.* Exeter, NH: Heinemann Education Books, 1983.

Hancock, Joelie, and Susan Hill. *Literature Based Reading Programs at Work.* Portsmouth, NH: Heinemann, 1988.

Hansen, Jane. *Breaking Ground.* Portsmouth, NH: Heinemann, 1985.

Hansen, Jane. *When Writers Read.* Portsmouth, NH: Heinemann, 1987.

Henderson, Edmund H., and James W. Beers, ed. *Developmental and Cognitive Aspects of Learning to Spell.* Newark, DE: International Reading Association, 1980.

Hornsby, David. *Read On: A Conference Approach to Reading.* Portsmouth, NH: Heinemann, 1988.

Huck, Charlotte S. *Children's Literature in Elementary School.* New York: Holt Reinhart, Winston, 1987.

Newkirk, Thomas, and Nanci Atwell, eds. *Understanding Writing.* Portsmouth, NH: Heinemann, 1986.

Parry, Jo Ann, and David Hornsby. *Write One: A Conference Approach to Writing.* Portsmouth, NH: Heinemann, 1988.

Temple, Ruth G. Nathon, and Nancy A. Burris. *The Beginnings of Writing*. Boston: Allyn and Bacon, 1982.

Trelease, Jim. *The Read Aloud Handbook*. New York: Penguin Books (Viking Press), 1982.

ay. Reading, MA: Addison-Wesley, 1976.

IA: Addison-Wesley, 1988.

. Reading, MA: Addison-Wesley, 1987.

Co. of America, Inc. *The Elementary Science Study* -Hill.

shington, D.C.: NAEYC, 1974.

Nashua, N.H.: Delta Education.

y

v York: Warner, 1989.

Wrong Grade. Rosemont, NJ: Programs for Education, 1987.

n This Grade? Rosemont, NJ: Programs for Education, 1985.

m I'm Difficult? Rosemont, NJ: Programs for Education, 1986.

Ask: Straight Answers from Louise Bates Ames. New York:

ers. *The Child From Five to Ten*. rev. ed. New York: Harper

uise Bates Ames. *Infant and Child in the Culture of Today*. 1974.

New York: Windmill Paperbacks, 1971.

lhood. New York: Pantheon, 1983.

NOTES: